THE
THERAPIST'S
EMOTIONAL
SURVIVAL

THE
THERAPIST'S
EMOTIONAL
SURVIVAL

DEALING WITH THE PAIN
OF EXPLORING TRAUMA

STUART D. PERLMAN, Ph.D.

JASON ARONSON INC.
Northvale, New Jersey
London

This book was set in 11 pt. Garamond and printed and bound by Book-mart Press, Inc. of North Bergen, New Jersey.

Library of Congress Cataloging-in-Publication Data

Perlman, Stuart D.
    The therapist's emotional survival : dealing with the pain of
exploring trauma / Stuart D. Perlman.
      p. cm.
    Includes bibliographical references and index.
    ISBN 0-7657-0175-8
    1. Post-traumatic stress disorder—Treatment.
2. Psychotherapists—Job stress. 3. Countertransference
(Psychology) I. Title.
    [DNLM: 1. Countertransference (Psychology) 2. Physician-Patient
Relations. 3. Stress Disorders, Post-Traumatic—therapy. 4. Child
Abuse, Sexual—psychology. WM 62 P451t 1999]
RC552.P67P45 1999
616.89'14—DC21
DNLM/DLC
for Library of Congress   98–23701

Printed in the United States of America on acid-free paper. For information and catalog write to Jason Aronson Inc., 230 Livingston Street, Northvale, New Jersey 07647-1726. Or visit our website: http://www.aronson.com

*To my wife Denise
and children David and Aaron,
who are all never-ending sources
of joy and support*

Contents

Acknowledgments

I thank George Atwood, Ph.D., for his faith and enthusiasm, without which I could not have written this book. I thank my patients, who have taught me and who gave permission for me to use their material. I thank the seminar groups at the Institute of Contemporary Psychoanalysis and at the Southern California Psychoanalytic Institute for reading and discussing drafts of this book. Some of the many colleagues who read and commented on this book are Louis Breger, Ph.D., Victoria Hamilton, Ph.D., Jane Rubin, Psy.D., Veronica Abney, M.S.W., Ann Isaacs, L.C.S.W., Joel Isaacs, Ph.D., Peter Maduro, and Estelle Shane, Ph.D. I especially thank my wife, Denise Gerber, who edits almost every word I write. I thank Victoria Kuhl, Michael Moskowitz, Ph.D., Elaine Lindenblatt, and Kitty Moore for their editorial help as well, and David Markel, M.D., for his input on the treatment process.

Introduction

Treating sexually abused and traumatized patients has tested my ability to manage my own emotions and has been a pressurized experience. These disrupted patients appear to need therapists to understand the pain they feel on a daily basis. I hope by sharing my experiences, I will help other therapists and patients to more effectively bridge the gap between them. The following internal dialogue begins to present the central issues. It also illustrates how I have used insight and self-analysis to explore and manage my experience with such patients.

As I sit waiting for my patient, my stomach feels edgy and my teeth are clenched. Exploring these sensations in self-analysis in the past, I have found fear, anger, and a sense of doom. What comes to mind at this moment is that these feelings have been triggered by the patient's message on my answering machine, telling me she is going to kill herself. How can she keep threatening to kill herself when I have gotten so attached to and involved with her? I sit with these feelings and explore further how this patient is affecting me. What emerges is a recurrent childhood dream familiar from my own psychotherapy:

My younger sister is falling into a dark, bottomless well, probably to her death. I grab her hand. I'm holding her hand with all my might but she is slipping away. I wake up distraught.

The patient's message feels like the relationship with my sister in the dream. One of my sorrows is that I could not save my sister and that inability is part of my motivation in treating traumatized and abused patients. I realize that I am confusing my patient with my sister. This is a relief.

I continue exploring. Each of these patients is in part my sister to me. I knew this before but had forgotten it. Each patient I treat is some penance for not saving her. This is a new realization. I could not save her from my parents when they went into violent rages. My sister has lived out this emotional damage. The adult side of me says, "I was just a child and not responsible." This makes me feel less guilty. The memories of insights from my original analysis soothe me as my original analyst did. I feel less responsible for the patient's suicide threat. I feel proud that I could do this piece of self-analysis and calm down.

Later, when I see the patient, she has switched to a different emotional state, one that is more hopeful and businesslike. Yet I am still reverberating from her earlier phone message.

The thought of my sister falling down the well returns, and I realize the patient has come to represent the needy child part of myself. I fear I would lose myself if this patient were to die. Others have not survived the traumas of childhood, yet I have been selfish enough to go on and have a better life.

My own unresolved baggage has been overloading my reactions to this patient's intense but shifting affect states.

This example illustrates the use of my own dreams, memories, and self-analysis to understand my work with traumatized patients. Like many therapists, I hoped that by studying psychology and helping others to heal, I would learn to heal myself and enhance my understanding of people. My personal therapy and analysis revolutionized my life. This book is an attempt to give something back to the field. It is also an attempt to help hurt and damaged individuals to improve their emotional states and levels of function. I am deeply touched by my patients' pain and inspired by their courage and fortitude, as well as by the many therapists who help these patients. One purpose of the literature on abuse is to break the silence that is part of the original trauma; speaking out is intrinsic to the healing process. The many patients who have given me permission to use their personal material in this book have been motivated by the desire to reveal their experience.

Another goal of this book is to help therapists accept their own experience as useful in understanding the bewildering process of treating severely traumatized and sexually abused patients. During the therapy process there will be periods of not understanding what is happening in the patient and in the treatment. During these periods, feelings and thoughts will percolate inside the therapist and patient that might only later be understood.

A central task for therapists is to learn how to process their own feelings about their patients without getting stuck in guilt, shame, or self-punitiveness. Therapists can understand and learn what to expect of themselves, and to detect the warning signals that indicate that their reactions and concomitant dynamics need attention. They can begin to contain their inner process and use it to enhance the treatment.

The ultimate goal of treatment is to create a new existence for the patient. Yet the treatment can also profoundly change the therapist. Because of this, the therapist needs empathy and support to enable him or her to make these changes. Usually, this empathy comes from the therapist's therapist, supervisors, and colleagues. One analyst told me that he finds rereading my papers soothing in the middle of the night, when he feels overwhelmed by the material presented by some of his patients. I hope that this book will serve as a similar guide for therapists who engage in this challenging work.

If the therapist is prepared with a map and support, there is more of a chance that the process will deepen with less strain. The map presented in this book is one that I, and those that I have supervised, have found useful, and one that fits with the choices I have made regarding levels of emotional availability to my patients.

This book can be read on different levels. First, it explores the therapist–patient interaction, with descriptions of what is triggered in each person as the treatment proceeds. I use myself as well as my patients for the purpose of case illustration. On another level, this is a book about the psychotherapeutic process; it presents a conceptualization of treatment, involving a series of developmental stages and tasks that the patient and therapist probably need to navigate together. This developmental view of treatment is especially tailored to traumatized people, but could be applicable to others as well. I have focused primarily on the therapist's feelings, and the interlocking dramas in which the therapist and patient often become enmeshed. Both the patient's and the therapist's phenomenological perspectives are described. The openings to deeper experience and treatment are explored. Patients who have been traumatized tend to re-create their traumas in the treatment, and the therapist needs to learn about and contain this.

I draw on over twenty years' experience in treating and supervising the treatment of many sexually abused and traumatized victims. The interactions between my patients and me are examined as they have changed over the years. The reader is given a glimpse of how therapeutic issues can be encountered in the therapeutic process, and how treatment may change patient and therapist. This book weaves together these different levels of experience into a guide for the journey with the patient in treatment, and the possible impact of this work on the therapist.

PART I

THE
PATIENT–THERAPIST
RELATIONSHIP

Part I, "The Patient–Therapist Relationship," gives an overview of the interplay between patient and therapist, including the mutual shaping, sensitivities, and individual histories that influence each person. How the field developed this awareness and then how I learned about these influences are the main focus of this first part of the book.

Chapter 1, "Pioneers," presents a historical survey of some of the pioneers who have laid the foundation for our ability to discuss treatment of abused and traumatized patients. Their personal struggles with these issues are instructive both in their contributions and missteps. Chapter 2, "The Survivor's Shattered Existence," offers an overview of the literature, both clinical and research, and some controversies in the field, as well as the symptoms of abuse and trauma survivors. Chapter 3, "Bearing the Pain of Treatment," highlights the difficulty of managing the intense countertransferences, crises, and stress of work with these patients. Chapter 4, "My Introduction to Treating Sexually Abused and Traumatized Patients," recounts my own formative experiences in learning to contain the treatment process—how my childhood experiences kept intruding into the treatment and how I eventually learned to use my emotional reactions to enhance treatment. Chapter 5, "Therapist Rescue Fantasies," probes one of the most difficult countertransferences: how the therapist's natural desire to save his patient from pain can both be facilitative but also pull the therapist out of role and interfere with the treatment process. Chapter 6, "Therapy Openings," presents the concept of openings to deeper experience in treatment. These openings are critical doorways to the exploring of traumatic material and hidden aspects of a person's experience that are necessary for deep healing.

CHAPTER 1

Pioneers

This personality, shattered and made defenseless by suffering and poison, is attempting, over and over again but always unsuccessfully, to reassemble its various parts into a unit, that is, to understand the events taking place in and around her . . . . However, the obstacles and amnesia in the analyst himself have delayed the emergence of an understanding (in the analyst; see her complaints about my erroneous judgments), and only now, as I begin to realize my mistakes and recognize and exonerate her as an innocent and well-intentioned person (I did in fact describe her in the most favorable terms at S.I.'s recently), are we approaching the possibility of fitting the fragments of her personality together and of enabling her, not only indirectly but also directly, to recognize and remember the actual fact and the causes of this disintegration. [Ferenczi 1932, pp. 158–159]

JANET, BREUER, AND FREUD

The above entry from Ferenczi's diary described his interaction with one of his trauma and abuse patients. It is no accident that new discoveries in psychoanalysis were developed by clinicians who treated sexually abused and traumatized patients. Both Freud and Janet studied in France during the 1880s. Here each saw the famous Charcot, who, while working with hysterics and hypnosis in front of large audiences, would hypnotize a paralyzed patient and the symptom would remit. Each took Charcot's work in different directions. Janet (1889) proposed the concept of dissociation as the centerpiece of the pathological process. Davies and Frawley (1994) summarized Janet's work as follows:

> Pierre Janet . . . first linked trauma and dissociation almost 100 years ago. Janet believed that memory was an act of creative integration by which human beings organized, encoded, and categorized experiences into already existing cognitive schemata . . . . Here is the early precursor of Piaget's bipolar dialectic between assimilation and accommodation. When an event in a person's life was too bizarre, terrifying, or overstimulating to fit into such preexisting schemata, Janet believed that it was split off from consciousness into a separate system of "fixed ideas." . . . There they became incorporated into their own system of organization, untouched or unmodulated by the rest of the individual's experience. [p. 31]

Similarly, Breuer (Breuer and Freud 1893–1895) conceived of patients becoming ill from trauma, sexual and otherwise. The traumatic experiences created altered states of consciousness, ego dissociation, splitting, and hypnoid states similar to the dissociation observed by Janet. Breuer conceived of the "talking cure," in which catharsis would free the patient from trauma, reintegrating it into the personality. In treating his case "Anna O.," Breuer was frightened by the patient's intense feelings toward him, and he withdrew from the treatment.

Evolving beyond his collaboration with Breuer, Freud (1887–1902, 1896a–c) espoused the seduction theory, in which he stated that the shock of intense sexual stimulation in childhood, often the result of incest or molestation by family members, and other traumas, specifically causes hysteria. Freud postulated that the energy resulting from a trauma remains trapped in the psyche and can be encoded as hysterical bodily manifestations. The psychic energy and affects became trapped due to conflict between drives and morality. Freud conceived of the topographic model, with repression's horizontal splitting of consciousness, where unacceptable ideas were banished to the unconscious. Freud stated that these ideas must be brought to consciousness; insight as a result of interpretation of the trauma would result in "cures" of the symptom.

Freud found that to understand the process, he needed to explore not only the patient's but also his own associations in his self-analysis (Breger 1981, Freud 1900). Freud's goal was to create a unified scientific project to explain the human psyche. His faith in the objective science of psychoanalysis dominated his approach to theory and clinical work.

Freud moved to a theory of oedipal desires and fantasies. He believed that the child's instinctual desires to have sex with the parent was being expressed in hysteria. His new theory de-emphasized actual experience and trauma as etiologic agents of pathology. He proposed that by interpreting the instincts and their conflict with the ego and superego, patients could develop conscious control of their lives.

Some critics have speculated that Freud switched from the seduction to the oedipal fantasy theory as a result of public reaction against the notion that fathers sexually abused their children (Masson 1984). Other writers have emphasized other reasons. However, even Masson, one of Freud's most ardent critics, nevertheless views Freud as periodically returning to the seduction theory.

FERENCZI

Ferenczi openly listened to his patients articulate their feelings and their critiques of him (Miller 1993, Rachman 1989). He began to experiment with new techniques because he believed the "classical" method did not work (Ferenczi 1932, 1933). Ferenczi returned to Breuer's concept of the "talking cure," whereby patients begin healing by having therapists listen to their pain.

Ferenczi (1933) broke with Freud in part over the centrality of trauma in the etiology of psychopathology. Ferenczi identified sexual abuse as rampant. He described the splitting and dissociative states that victims use to survive, and how they become crystallized in the personality. These splits can be so deep as to separate the personality into individuals organized separately unto themselves. Ferenczi discussed the "confusion of tongues" between the victim and the abuser: the victim seeks love, and the perpetrator interprets this as sexual passion. Ferenczi pointed out that similar confusion can arise between the patient and the analyst. He was the first to highlight that the lack of empathy could be traumatic; parents who use their children to meet their own narcissistic needs rob them of their sense of self (Ferenczi 1933).

Ferenczi argued for a more genuine emotional encounter between patient and therapist. In his *Clinical Diary* and other works, Ferenczi (1932) describes the patient's need for his or her therapist's openness and honesty, even recommending that the therapist admit foibles and mistakes. He believed that for therapists to be cold and distant, or to deny the accuracy of a patient's perceptions, was to retraumatize the patient. Rachman (1989) summarized Ferenczi's contributions to therapeutic process as follows:

> The advances Ferenczi's work represents can be listed under three basic headings:
>
> 1. The issue of "professional hypocrisy," questioning the traditional analytic stance as unempathic and traumatic.
>
> 2. The creation of a corrective emotional experience and democratic atmosphere where empathy prevails.
>
> 3. The employment of four techniques to maintain an empathic stance in the analysis: (a) analysis of countertransference to "rock bottom"; (b) the development of "mutual analysis"; (ç) a fuller analysis of the analyst—periodic return to analysis; (d) therapist self-disclosure. [p. 188]

BRITISH MIDDLE SCHOOL

Balint brought Ferenczi's (1933) work to England, having translated and published it in English. Ferenczi's work fit with the ideas of the British psychoanalytic middle school. This middle school took a center position between the work of Melanie Klein and that of Anna Freud, both of whom thought they were representing Freud.

One of the voices in this school, Winnicott (1947), described the powerful feelings that therapists may have when treating traumatized and disturbed patients:

> It is important to study the ways in which anxiety of psychotic quality and also hate are produced in those who work with severely ill psychiatric patients. Only in this way can there be any hope of the avoidance of therapy that is adapted to the needs of the therapist rather than to the needs of the patient. [p. 203]

Winnicott emphasized the need for therapists to contain their own feelings, as well as those of the patient. He used the analogy of the "good-enough mother" to describe the therapist who can be there sufficiently for patients, and who allows them to develop their ability to be themselves. In his paper, "The Capacity to Be Alone," Winnicott (1972a) described how the presence of the therapist can be supportive of his or her patients' needs, even when the therapist is silent.

In the United States at this time, Searles (1955, 1975) discussed many of these issues in the context of American classical theory and the study of countertransference. He emphasized how therapists can use their feelings to understand the dynamics of treatment interaction. He also emphasized the importance of understanding the patients' enactments with their therapists and the therapists' enactments with their supervisors. He took these ideas further, although he did not develop a theory to encompass his insights.

> Among man's most powerful strivings toward his fellow men, beginning in the earliest years and even earliest months of life, is an essentially psychotherapeutic striving . . . . The patient is ill because, and to the degree that, his own psychotherapeutic strivings have been subjected to such vicissitudes that they have been rendered inordinately intense; frustrated of fulfillment or even acknowledgment; admixed therefore with unduly intense components of hate, envy and competitiveness; and subjected, therefore, to repression. In transference terms, the patient's illness expresses his unconscious attempt

to cure the doctor . . . . The more ill a patient is, the more does his successful treatment require that he become, and be implicitly acknowledged as having become, a therapist to his officially designated therapist, the analyst. [Searles 1975, pp. 95–96]

SELF PSYCHOLOGY, INTERPERSONAL PSYCHOLOGY, AND INTERSUBJECTIVITY

The field of psychoanalysis in the United States produced several groups of theorists emphasizing the interaction of two subjective individuals in the therapeutic process. These groups include the intersubjectivists (Stolorow et al. 1987), interpersonalists (Greenberg and Mitchell 1983, Sullivan 1953), and self psychologists (Goldberg 1992, Kohut 1971, 1977, 1984, Lichtenberg 1983, Shane et al. 1997). These theorists take the therapist's inner experience into account in their theories of the therapeutic process. Stolorow and Atwood (1979), in their book *Faces in a Cloud*, state that the theorists' childhood experiences and resulting personality structures and defenses influence the basic premises of their theory of psychotherapy. To go one step further, I would add that aspects of treatment are determined both consciously by the therapists' beliefs and unconsciously by their own traumatic experiences.

These pioneers groped through the darkness of not knowing, and were willing to explore their own and their patients' feelings to bring new insights. Each in their own way listened to and learned from their patients. Their courage to endure through uncertainty, and to openly explore their own and their patients' complex and painful experiences, needs to be a model for the therapist attempting to treat sexually abused and traumatized patients.

These pioneers deepened our understanding of therapy and paved the way for contemporary writers. As a result, a two-person psychology has become more prevalent in the psychoanalytic zeitgeist. Some mainstream thinkers in traditional psychoanalysis who have a body of work in two-person psychology are Leo Stone, Merton Gill, James McLaughlin, Owen Renik, and Ted Jacobs. These writers have enriched our understanding of countertransference, self-disclosure, and abstinence.

In the treatment of sexually abused and traumatized patients, Davies and Frawley (1992a, 1994) utilize this approach. They explain how patients pull their therapists into an enactment of their personal dramas as a way to bring the deep pain of the past into the therapeutic arena. It is this enactment and drama that open up the patient's cutoff pain, allowing it to be reworked in treatment. These authors stress that enactments are not evidence of poor treatment, but rather are necessary to retrieve and work on traumatic material that is unavailable to consciousness.

CHAPTER 2

The Survivor's Shattered Existence

Ferenczi (1933) described the child's reaction to trauma, specifically sexual abuse, as follows:

It is difficult to imagine the behavior and the emotions of children after such violence . . . . These children feel physically and morally helpless; their personalities are not sufficiently consolidated in order to be able to protest, even if only in thought, for the overpowering force and authority of the adult makes them dumb and can rob them of their senses. The same anxiety, however, if it reaches a certain maximum, compels them to subordinate themselves like automata to the will of the aggressor, to divine each one of his desires and to gratify these; completely oblivious of themselves, they identify themselves with the aggressor. [p. 162]

Many authors (Briere 1992a, Davies and Frawley 1992a, 1994, Finkelhor et al. 1990, Herman 1992, Kluft 1984, 1991, Krystal 1988, Levine 1990, Putnam 1989, Russell 1984, Shengold 1989, Terr 1991, van der Kolk and Fisler 1994, Van der Kolk et al. 1996) have described the needs, behavior patterns, and traits of these abused and traumatized patients. I will highlight a few of the basic ideas and controversies in the field.

In trauma theory, there is a controversy about whether to use a broad or narrow definition of the term *trauma*, that is, whether the definition should be delimited to experiences that would be extremely stressful to most people or to experiences defined as traumatic based only on a person's subjective experience. Hamilton (1989) urges a narrow definition, so that the term does not lose its meaning. She asserts that for an experience to be defined as trauma it must meet the following criteria: an event or events that most persons would experience as traumatic, that haunts the person in the present, and that acts as a psychic organizer. I use this narrow definition of trauma, abuse, and sexual abuse, emphasizing its more extreme forms.

Herman (1992) suggests that the following factors increase a victim's experience of helplessness and terror, which is then related to the extent of symptoms: being taken by surprise, trapped, or exposed to the point of exhaustion; experiencing physical violation, injury, or exposure to violence; or witnessing gruesome death. She emphasizes the following symptoms of trauma: intense terror; hyperarousal; intrusive recollections or flashbacks; constriction or numbing and trances; and feelings of disconnection from others, community, and faith.

Terr's (1991) definition is similar to Herman's, though she adds that these patients have a syndrome of repetitive memories of the traumatic event; behavioral repetition of the trauma; trauma-specific fears; and changed attitudes about people, life, and the future. Terr sees a difference in survivors' symptoms according to whether the trauma was a single discrete event in time, such as a car accident, or a repeated trauma, like daily child abuse. In single-event trauma, the patient has full, detailed memories, omens of the trauma, and misperceptions of reexperience; in repetitive trauma, the patient has symptoms of denial and numbing, self-hypnosis, dissociation, and rage.

The assumption that patients can remember previously unremembered or unreported sexual abuse is supported by the research literature and is central to the treatment process described in this book. Along these lines, Briere (1992b) conducted a survey that found that the inability to remember sexual abuse was correlated with early onset and degree of violence. Williams (1992) obtained similar results with methodologically stronger research. In her study, children were examined in the emergency room of the hospital where they were brought for medical assistance. The sexual abuse was medically documented at that time and recorded. Ten to twelve years later the same victims were followed up and asked to participate in a health study. In an extensive interview, a number of questions were asked regarding abuse in childhood. More than one-third of the victims were unable to recall the documented abuse. Some reported other abuse, but a full 17 percent did not remember or report any abuse.

Van der Kolk and Fisler (1994) agree with the symptoms delineated by Herman and Terr, but conceptualize the primary effect of trauma as dysregulation of both biological and emotional needs. They view neglect, which is involved in many situations of chronic trauma, as having a broader blanketing effect on the overall personality than specific traumas.

Davies and Frawley (1992a, 1994) indicate, as did Janet (1889), that sudden shifts in emotional state and dissociation are the primary symptoms and coping styles of traumatized patients. They emphasize that separated or dissociated states of functioning and memory need to be spoken to directly in treatment, especially in the case of sexual abuse and trauma.

The victim's personality structure and developmental level of the person when the trauma occurred is weighted differently by theorists. Freud (1896c) believed that all hysteria and other forms of psy- chopathology were the result of trauma that occurred before the age of 8. He believed that these early experiences create a template for future psychopathology. Freud at that time argued that it is not present stress but the patient's early experiences and constitution that determined the type and extent of the symptoms. In contrast, some contemporary theorists emphasize the characteristics of the current event more than the survivor's history or early experience. For example, Herman (1992) believes that the intensity of the traumatic event is directly correlated to the degree of psychopathology. In her view even well-integrated persons, if exposed to strong enough stressors, will exhibit the basic symptoms of trauma. Terr (1991) goes even further, indicating that the characteristics of the trauma will re-create symptoms specific to the original experience.

Miller (1981, 1983) emphasizes the importance of support from caregivers after the trauma as crucial to the repair and lasting effect of trauma. Stolorow (1994) goes even further, making the support that enables affective integration of the trauma the most important factor in the long-term effect of the trauma.

Severe cases of violent and repetitive early trauma exhibit the most dissociation and disruptive symptoms. Severe early trauma creates split-off or dissociated experiences, terror, disconnection, and fear of other people, including the therapist. I have come to believe that if therapists can understand and learn to treat these more severe and complex traumatic states, they can begin to recognize the subtler effects of traumas. Without understanding the more dramatic effects, they often miss more subtle ones. Most patients display a broad range of symptoms, based on their social context and current level of stress, and the reaction of caregivers to the trauma and symptoms.

PATIENTS

A more experiential description can help integrate these research and theoretical conclusions for the reader. Severely traumatized patients who come to treatment still have some hope. Most of them speak on many levels about their hopes, dreads, and traumas as they search for ways to feel safe, to be heard, and to achieve integration. These patients usually have a history of trying to heal themselves. There may have been attempts to accomplish these goals through the use of drugs and alcohol, self-mutilation, sexual and emotional enslavement, withdrawal, masturbation, adrenaline addiction, suicide attempts, and clinging to other people. Therapy can also be another of these attempts.

Severe trauma patients have found a way to survive. Some try to protect themselves by vigilance, some by not knowing and not experiencing the unbearable, and some by walling off the unacceptable and protecting themselves. Without these adaptations, they would be overwhelmed. These adaptations were often developed in the absence of a supportive environment that would have allowed the pain to be heard and integrated.

These patients, and the hidden parts that have been traumatized, are often asking, "Is it safe enough to exist?" or "Is it safe enough to experience who I am and have someone else know of my existence?" These questions are asked in many ways, as discussed in Part II of this book. Real dangers and abuse may still exist in their adult lives and be life threatening, and thus need to be taken seriously.

In addition, these patients may be haunted and terrorized by shattering experiences that have occurred in the past, versions of which may recur at any moment. This threat may progressively overwhelm them and destroy their connection with the outer world. The original trauma may have been too overwhelming for the patients' cognitive and emotional structure to handle, leaving them frozen and disconnected from others.

Many dramas and problems that survivors bring to treatment are enactments that contain the traumatic residue (Davies and Frawley 1992a, 1994, Terr 1991). Such residue needs to be worked through, so that the split-off or repressed parts of the self can be integrated. This traumatic residue may not be accessible to verbal memory systems. Accessing nonverbal body memories, which more recently have been called "procedural memory" (Clyman 1992, Squire 1986, 1987), offers the therapist an opening to the deeper, more dissociated parts of the patient's self (Perlman 1993, 1995, 1996a,b). In turn, therapists can have their own procedural memories or dissociated parts triggered within the treatment process. Therapists may then feel compelled to behave and participate within the therapeutic context in ways that are determined by their past and not by the treatment needs of the patient.

CHAPTER 3

Bearing the Pain of Treatment

Some therapists are drawn to this profession in the hope that if they ✳
care for others, they will be cared for in return. They often have
their own traumatic histories. The work may be a way to manage
their childhood pain. No matter how disguised these needs are, they
are always present, and usually come to consciousness when the
patient touches on related material. As Winnicott (1947) suggested,
the therapist is usually cued to the existence of such unmet needs by
the experience of anxiety and anger toward the patient. More than
any other patients I have worked with, sexual abuse and trauma survivors provoke deep emotional responses and raise unresolved issues
in the therapist. Often the therapist and patient are reliving their
respective traumas at the same time in the session. That is why it is
so important to illuminate the process of managing and exploring the
therapist's own experience in the context of the patient's treatment.

Legacies of the therapist's early, perhaps traumatic, experiences
interact with the needs, fears, and behaviors of the traumatized and
abused patient. Two traits therapists commonly bring to the treatment process are the needs to help others and to demonstrate competence. Usually there is some investment in being a good, caring

person, along with an ego ideal of not hurting others. Therapists usually have some investment in being able to process and contain their own emotions. All these investments can be challenged in the treatment process with traumatized and abused patients.

RECURRENT ISSUES IN THE TREATMENT OF TRAUMATIZED AND ABUSED PATIENTS

Safety

Schafer (1983) states that the primary task of therapists is to establish and maintain a safe, trusting environment. This is especially difficult with sexually abused and traumatized patients because of their sense of being betrayed, disconnected from others, and haunted by the fear of trauma's recurrence (Herman 1992). More generally, their awareness of the destructive potential of other people makes them fear therapists.

Patients must come to feel that therapists are trying, in good faith, to be present with them in the fullest sense, looking honestly at what is going on with the patient and within themselves. This is especially important for trauma patients, many of whom have been rejected and not listened to. Therapists need to be open to acknowledge and discuss what occurs so that patients do not feel as if their reality has once again been ignored or invalidated. There needs to be a commitment to see and hear patients for who they are, and to stay with them through the experience. With trauma survivors, therapists may need to connect to the traumatized or dissociated child part of patients, until the child can be released from captivity. This places difficult demands on therapists in a treatment process that can also involve therapists in emotionally destructive dramas.

Connection

Many of these patients have been traumatized and betrayed by others, which can intensify hypervigilance and sensitivity to the emotional states of others. Paradoxically, these patients may be extremely accurate readers of others' emotional processes while remaining disconnected from them. As a result of this sensitivity, most of these patients require genuine and congruent emotional reactions from therapists.

Patients need contact with the emotional core of therapists while they are in the throes of reliving their trauma. The original trauma may have been too cognitively and emotionally overwhelming, leaving patients frozen in their internal experience, disconnected from others. Therapists' and patients' automatic response to such trauma or its vivid reexperience is usually to flee, fight, or freeze. To stay present, therapists may have to face the terror that patients' material triggers in them. Therapists remaining present can provide a context within which patients reintegrate the trauma and reestablish connections to others. It gives a person who has been mistreated, betrayed, or disappointed the chance to experience the conflicts, emotions, and humanity of another and to work out a relationship.

Interruptive Behavior and Tolerances

One of the most difficult experiences in treatment for both patient and therapist to tolerate is the ambiguity of not knowing what is real and what may be imagined or fantasy. This is particularly a problem with sexually abused and traumatized patients. Not knowing what is real, what affects and behaviors mean, and whether the therapist has the psychic stamina to manage his or her own and the patient's affects and memories presents a moment-to-moment struggle in the therapeutic process. As therapy progresses, both participants monitor the other's ability to tolerate going deeper into the patient's material. If either one cannot, he or she will interrupt the treatment. For example, the therapist might ask disruptive questions or change the topic. If one listens to a tape recording of a session, these interruptions often become obvious, though they may occur without either participant being aware of them.

Boundaries

In trauma, people often experience their boundaries being violated. Their sense of control is stripped away, and they are forced into states of helplessness and terror. They may psychically escape internally. Many patients' bodies have been violated so many times that they experience themselves as living solely in their head, or they leave and live outside their body. These patients feel they have no power or choice. They then attempt to set up relationships based on these boundary concepts, which they replicate in their relationships with the therapist. Helping these patients rebuild appropriate boundaries requires exquisite attention to the issue of self-ownership, to how patients experience both themselves and the therapist.

Enactments and Dramas

Work with traumatized patients frequently involves emotional enactments. An enactment is a repetition of an earlier experience, or of an important new dynamic related to an early experience, usually without consciousness. These enactments are dramas acted out with the therapist, many times with the therapist's full emotional involvement. If the therapist becomes emotionally caught up in these dramas, it does not mean that the treatment has gone awry. Davies and Frawley (1992a, 1994) eloquently discuss this issue. For enactments to occur in a constructive way, the therapist must face his or her own feelings and actions that resemble aspects of the patient's abuse or trauma. What is occurring in the treatment must be explored at some point. Aspects of the therapist's early history may be reactivated, which under most other circumstances would have lain dormant. This is an opportunity and a danger for both therapist and patient.

Intensity of the Therapeutic Relationship

The intensity of deep, long-term treatment and its eventual delimited intimacy can be as intense as a marriage or, at times, a parent–child relationship. As in marriage, it is crucial that each partner remain committed to working on the relationship. Each participant may have strong reactions to the depth of the other's emotions and behaviors over a long history of deep and frequent interactions. Sometimes the patient enters the psyche of the therapist to be carried around like a fetus in the womb of the therapist's mind, gestating until psychic rebirth occurs. Bromberg (1994) discusses this process as well. At the same time, the therapeutic relationship is different than a marriage or parent–child relationship. In a marriage the relationship is more equal and there are different areas to negotiate, such as sex and children, than in the delimited therapeutic relationship. In the parent–child relationship the parent is more financially, legally, and physically responsible for the child than the therapist, whose responsibility is primarily emotional and professional.

Strains on the Therapist's Coping Resources

Treating people who have survived severe trauma and sexual abuse can confront the therapist with his or her own limits, needs, and emotions. Some patients present the therapist with suicide attempts, self-mutilation, terror-laden late-night calls, emotional and physical intrusions, sexualized feelings, intense attachments, multiple personalities, and repressed memories. All these phenomena can stimulate intense emotions in the therapist.

These emotions can undermine the therapist's self-regulation, and erode or even destroy the supports and boundaries of the professional setting. The therapist can become so preoccupied by the patient's disturbing material that the therapist may have nightmares or be unable to relax when away from the office. The therapist may be haunted by what patients have reported and acted out, and worry about what might happen next. Unexamined, these burdens can build in the therapist, potentially erupting as destructive acting out toward patients.

Many of these patients have developed sensitive antennae that alert them to possible danger, and they may be specifically attentive to the emotional states of authority figures. In an unwitting attempt to protect themselves from the intrusions of patients, the therapist may employ strategies such as denying the patients' experience, forcing patients into compliance, or pushing them out of treatment. Alternatively, the therapist may overextend him- or herself, trying to meet compelling concretized needs and wishes. The therapist may make

Herculean efforts to quell patients' fears, recapture the patients' lost childhood, and heal psychic wounds. Such overextensions can cause burnout, depression, physical symptoms, and damage to the therapist's personal relationships.

Therapists may need to contain the patients' fears by having an awareness of the full range of their own feelings and of the historical roots of such feelings. Therapists must continually monitor their own impact on the treatment. To do all of this, therapists need help.

Therapist's Need for Support

Given the strain of working with trauma survivors, therapists do well to obtain professional and personal support. Personally, therapists need enough love and attention from significant others, friends, family and/or their own therapy so that they do not turn to patients as a major source of sustenance. Without personal support, therapists are more vulnerable to being pulled into enacting inappropriate roles, and may have great difficulty working their way out of difficult situations.

Professionally, therapists need help identifying enactments and problems that may be unconscious. This help usually comes from instructors and supervisors, colleagues, and personal therapists.

Therapists who work with abused patients are often subject to criticism and hostile questioning (e.g., by colleagues and by the patient's family), which may evoke feelings similar to those experienced by the patients themselves. This makes it harder to maintain an open, believing orientation to the patient. Many questions arise when this material is presented in professional settings. The questions may be quite direct such as, "Don't you think you might be putting these ideas into the patient's head?" or "Aren't these just a borderline's fantasies?" Out of fear of criticism, both patients and therapists may tend to avoid presenting this material to others, even supportive others. When this happens, both therapist and patient are cutting themselves off from sources of support.

A supportive environment inside and outside of treatment is needed to discuss the material that inevitably arises in the treatment of traumatized individuals. In such an environment the feelings of both parties can be explored, including their doubts about the veracity of memories of abuse, without endangering connections to all-important colleagues, mentors, family, and friends. Patients experience difficult cycles of belief and disbelief about their abuse. Increasing the complexity is the fact that the therapist, too, may go through such cycles. Many of these reactions can be repetitions of the reactions of others in the patient's (and therapist's) past or present.

ILLUSTRATIONS OF RECURRENT ISSUES

Patients are typically very sensitive to therapists' emotional reactions and may feel pressured to satisfy their needs and wishes (Ferenczi 1933). It is the responsibility of therapists to track these currents and remain focused on the patients' interests.

Some issues and themes recur in treatment. The following clinical examples illustrate the dance between the needs and tolerances of patients and therapists, the nature and intensity of the experience of treatment, what is activated in therapists, and the importance of safety, connection, enactment, interruptive behavior, and boundaries. These illustrations emphasize the therapist's perspective, because that perspective is lacking in the literature. Later in the book, the focus shifts to the patient's perspective. Ann's ten-year treatment is used throughout the book to illustrate treatment issues. I have selected Ann as an example because, over the course of her treatment, she taught me a great deal about the needs of traumatized and sexually abused patients.

Ann

Ann was one of several children. Her father was in the military and the family followed him from one military base to another. Father was violent to mother and the children, and committed incest with and tortured Ann. Ann's parents divorced when she was 7. She was raised by her mother and did not see her father for several years. Mother struggled financially and father did not help. Mother never remarried.

Ann had seen five other therapists in the six years prior to approaching me. She experienced chronic lethargy and pain in her neck, throat, chest, and vaginal area, as well as difficulty swallowing. Looking back, she thought that her previous therapists in one way or another had suppressed her emerging memories. She had been diagnosed with chronic fatigue syndrome or Epstein-Barr virus by a series of physicians. Her work history was spotty. She is an artist and her drawings and art are revealing, especially since they are the product of her emotional struggles and dreams.

This chapter demonstrates the complexities of the therapeutic relationship by illustrating a few interactions in the opening months of treatment with Ann. The first issue, which recurs through this book, is how painful the patient's material can be and how the patient fears that the therapist will be overwhelmed and reject him or her or interfere with movement toward more painful states. Another theme is how intense and powerful the therapist's reactions can be for the patient.

During a very painful period of reliving of the violent incest she experienced as a child, Ann feared I would become overwhelmed. Offering me her coping strategy, she made a beautiful multicolored fan as a present for me to look at during sessions. When she had been brutally abused as a child, she would pick a pretty color and "disappear into it" as a way to survive. She told me about this skill. She was proud of her artwork and hoped I would appreciate it. She feared ridicule of her work and also the possibility that it would provoke me to some violence toward her, such as rape. I told her how very much I liked her art, that it was special to have a piece of it, and that I would use the fan to help me in our work together. I genuinely thanked her, making sure that she felt my appreciation for her art. I was happy that I had received a piece of her art, and hoped I might receive more some day.

I genuinely liked Ann. She was bright, interesting, sensitive, and earnest in trying to heal herself. My heart went out to her, and I could feel her liking for me. I was happy to be engaged in such an intimate experience with someone with whom I felt a natural rapport.

Her feelings of love and fear, her longing for closeness, and her dread stirred up reciprocal feelings in me. My desire for a piece of her art made me nervous. I was aware of that at the time I received the gift. She had brought in artwork before, and she told me that she had given a few pieces to friends as presents. I felt that I deserved a piece. When she did give me the art, I could sense the additional significance. Only years later did I realize, in exploring my own experience, that this had been a way of holding on to a piece of her. I had not wanted to face the possibility of getting close to her, and then losing the relationship. Yet this loss is embedded in the relationship of the psychotherapist and patient; it is a delimited intimacy, and loss looms as the patient gets better. I had come to enjoy my relationship with her, even while I hated listening to her horrible stories of abuse. At times, I was over-whelmed by her material, and wished she would leave.

A recurrent issue in treatment is the therapist's concerns about how others in the field will view their feelings and actions in treatment.

I accepted Ann's gift, but wondered what other therapists would think. In some circles, it is considered inappropriate to accept gifts from pa-tients. I thought about other experiences that I had, where what I felt was best for the patient was something that may have left me open to the negative judgment of others. I feared that psychoanalytic authori-ties would tell me I had broken an essential rule.

Another critical issue and theme discussed throughout this book is how much therapists need support in doing this work, and how, in the absence of such support, they attempt, inappropriately, to meet their emotional needs by turning to patients.

Later, trying to manage the strain of Ann's treatment, I was able to ex-plore my fear that her material would overwhelm me. I looked forward to supervision and my analysis to help me process my feelings. After each session I pondered how my childhood traumas were restimulated, how they sometimes would intrude in the sessions with Ann. I was sur-prised to discover that she was aware of my difficulties, as evidenced by her gift of the fan.

I hoped that this gift was concrete proof that Ann was grateful for what I was doing for her. Somehow, her being grateful was important to me. I felt taxed by her demands on my time and energy, and I wanted something beyond the reduced fee and her thanks to make it worth my while to go through so much painful material with her. Her gift concretized her gratitude.

Days later, I felt defensive when she expressed the idea that I could not manage the experience of hearing her material. I told myself, "I'm a seasoned therapist." At the same time, I was relieved that she knew I was having trouble, and I hoped that she might be considerate of my difficulties. I felt that she was saying to me, "I know you are having trouble and I will help you; here is the fan." I was able to continue treating Ann, in part because she periodically helped me over some rough spots. This mutual helping is one aspect of treatment that is overlooked in many descriptions of psychotherapy. It is especially crucial for these patients, since they were forced to sacrifice their own needs to care for the abuser. It is especially meaningful to them when their therapist acknowledges their efforts to help.

Another issue is how we as therapists cope with the profound needs of these patients. In the face of such intense trauma, some forms of therapist survivor guilt and rescue fantasies are almost inevitable.

Some months into treatment, Ann needed more frequent sessions because she was flooded with painful memories. She felt desperate; I had helped her open up, so I felt an obligation to provide the additional therapy time.

I also needed to have a training case for my requirements in my analytic education. I told her so, and proposed to see her more frequently at a further reduced fee rate if I could use her material in my educational activities and in my writing. On exploration, she seemed to like this idea because it made her feel special to me, knowing that I would spend hours in between sessions thinking about her.

My initial reaction to this agreement was one of relief. I obtained the training case that I needed, while at the same time meeting her needs. As part of my analytic training, this case was supervised weekly. What I needed and received from my supervisor was his reassurance that it was natural to have feelings in the face of so much human pain. I came to understand that I was not "bad" or "acting out," but simply feeling what anyone would. These feelings fit into a theoretical framework for self psychology, and could be described and discussed in supervision. Finding that the stance that I was using to treat Ann was permissible and supported by a theory was a great relief. Self psychology, in my supervisor's view, helped me treat Ann in a manner consistent with my own convictions.

I experienced Ann's deep desire to merge and become one with me. I found myself pulled closer emotionally by this. This opened me to experience her pain more intensely and motivated me to try to rescue her from the pain, as a parent tries to save a child from injury.

The immensity of these patients' pain and need provokes a feeling of inadequacy in the therapist. Unexamined, this sense of inadequacy can push the therapist into sacrifices that have not been thought through. Was I being dominated by these almost instinctual emotional reactions, which the depth of Ann's pain, along with her need for our connection, had activated? I wondered if I was enacting a desire to be a knight in shining armor, and save her. I sensed that she wanted a rescuer. Was that too compelling for me to resist? Was this rescue fantasy a way of avoiding the intensity of her pain?

Another issue that creates difficulty in treating these patients is the social and political controversy around trauma and abuse.

Years later, when I looked back on my agreement with Ann, I wondered how our work might look to others. I had heard about many lawsuits around the treatment of sexually abused patients. All of the legal problems and controversial headlines in the media aroused questions about my vulnerability to lawsuits. These questions precipitated other doubts. Was I taking advantage of a desperate person? Was it ethical, even with her consent, to write about a person in pain who desperately needed treatment but could not get it anywhere else at the frequency she needed, given her finances?

Another issue is how hard it is to stay clear about the relationship and its boundaries, about whose feelings are whose.

I thought Ann's art was very special. Was this because the art was really good, or was this more evidence of my overidentification with her?

I had wanted to be an artist when I was younger, but chose to be a therapist instead.

I experienced self doubts about my judgment. Was this caused by a mirroring of her states, or was it my own separate process, something akin to the chronic self-doubt so typical of the sexually abused patient? I had not been sexually abused, but I had grown up in a chaotic family with a mixture of violence and love. How did this history affect my perceptions of Ann?

Figure 3-1

Ann gave me a picture (Figure 3–1) as a gift in the opening months of the treatment. It illustrates the essentially interpersonal nature of the therapeutic process. On exploration a few sessions later she talked about her gratitude, the roads and ribbons to connect, and the walls that block such connection, as well as her feelings of hope and dread. Hope and frustration are ever present. She is sitting in the background and is also in the foreground facing me (with the beard).

I had many reactions to this picture when it was given to me. I was happy that I had obtained another piece of art. I experienced narcissistic gratification: she had made this one of me and especially for me. I also felt it was special that she could show her feelings about the therapeutic process in her art.

Finding solid ground in this relationship felt more difficult than with other patients. My feelings toward Ann were too strong; she seemed to test my boundaries.

I was aware of many questions at the time. Was it fair for me to accept another piece of art from her? I felt guilt and an internal struggle over this. On exploring my reactions I realized there were other issues contributing to this struggle. Even with the reduced fee, she was not paying her full bill each month. My anger grew over her unpaid bill, and guilt accompanied this anger. As both grew, I became more ashamed. I would discuss it with my supervisor, who would say, "Remember, it fulfills part of your educational requirements and that is a kind of payment." But this did not help. Did Ann know I was angry over the bill, and was the gift a way of keeping me from throwing her out of treatment? She reported feeling guilty and trapped in treatment. Was this about the money? Was she feeling guilt and anger, which were then transferred to me? What were the appropriate boundaries in this situation?

Another theme is the impact of the treatment on the therapist's family.

I wondered if I was giving Ann preferential treatment because she was an attractive young woman. She seemed to me more like a wounded child. Am I a pushover for the wounded child? Shouldn't I be more careful about the money, since my family has needs, too, and I'm seeing her five times per week at such a reduced fee? Who is exploiting whom?

I welcomed the weekly supervision of this case, because my supervisor was supportive and helped me to set limits.

A constant theme of this book is the feelings, including unresolved ones from childhood, that the patient's treatment can stir up in the therapist.

I continued to explore my reactions to these interactions for months, especially to Ann's gift of the fan. When I presented the case to a new supervisor, he suggested that the fan was a gift to ward off Ann's fear of me. The idea that her gift represented a reaction against the possibility that I might be violent toward her triggered my defenses. The supervisor insisted on this idea and I did not like it. I thought, "But I'm not violent. I am no rapist. I know this is transference, but please, this violates my self concept! On the other hand, don't I feel rage at times? When I was a kid, didn't I have fights? What about that sex play as a kid? Maybe she sees something inside me I'm not in touch with. No! I rebel against this sense of myself."

Years have passed, yet I continue to question the meanings of these interactions. Was my caring and dread too intense? What parts of Ann's treatment enacted her traumatic experiences and what parts enacted my own?

Over time, we discovered that her artwork usually depicted traumatic images of abuse, which she could remember only as she drew. To have rejected her gift would have been to reject her memories of the abuse in the form that she could show them to me.

Nine years into the analysis, I still have the fan in my office and still need to use it periodically. Somehow the fan has helped give me permission to be human and to retain my own feelings as I work with these patients.

These clinical examples illustrate some of the complex experiences the therapist needs to contain in work with patients such as Ann. They also show how the meanings of these interactions change over time. Meanings also change for patients, as the treatment progresses. I used personal reflection to uncover my own feelings. Rarely can more than a portion of the therapist's or patient's reactions be attended to at any moment. Most of these reactions remain unconscious.

There is an important boundary between therapist freedom and containment: one needs to have access to one's emotional reactions while remaining sensitive to the individual needs and sensitivities of patients. Some patients find it helpful when the therapist discloses his or her personal reactions while others feel used. These issues must be explored with each individual patient.

In this book I have frequently mentioned my own analysis and supervision. Especially with these difficult patients, most therapists will have a hard time maintaining their role without some emotional and clinical anchor outside of the treatment, such as peer supervision. Without such outside support, the patient and therapist can easily fall into collusion. They may repeat enactments from the past without ever exploring them, or the therapist's needs may intrude into the relationship in exploitative ways. The power of the therapist in the treatment dyad is great and must be monitored.

CHAPTER 4

My Introduction to Treating Sexually Abused and Traumatized Patients

A first step in treating traumatized and sexually abused patients is to accept the idea that such abuse and trauma occurs, in severe forms, and has possibly happened to this patient. Personal experiences, and the therapist's capacity to remember pain, prepares one to accept the pain of others. Patients' stories, and what one learns from others, create a readiness, as do the professional literature and the media.

FIRST PROFESSIONAL CONTACT

In graduate school, I was shocked to hear about the sexual abuse suffered by a friend. The following is a composite account of the first sexually abused patients I treated many years ago:

This was a case where the father's incest of the girl was clearly documented. As a result, the family was referred for treatment. I had difficulty fully believing that this father and mother were capable of such behavior. They then enacted aspects of the situation before my eyes. The mother seemed to be more interested in keeping a remnant of a relationship with her sexually abusive husband than she was in siding with her adolescent daughter or keeping her safe. This shocked me,

➤ but opened my eyes to the existence of uncaring parents and denial. What I was most aware of was my outrage that no one was taking care of this child. For the first time, I was allowing myself to feel angry at my own parents, especially my mother, for not protecting me and my siblings from my father. I did not make any connection between my anger at the parents of this adolescent and my anger at my parents. Countertransference was not a concept I was familiar with. My anger was experienced as totally about this family in treatment and this child. The sexual abuse in this family seemed a familiar treatment issue to my supervisor at a community clinic. The supervision did not deal at all with my feelings. I never connected fully with the girl and primarily worked at case management.

I then began to see more abuse among my patients and to be more aware of the feelings this material aroused in me.

Another family I treated contained violence and wife battering as well as child abuse. It was one of the first cases where I was aware that I was feeling overwhelmed, and I lost my sense of being protected as a therapist. The pain of the children and the crazed mother made me profoundly sad and upset. I now wonder if the pain and depression of those children reminded me of my own childhood sadness: my fear of an out-of-control angry mother and a violent father. But, at that time, I made no connections to myself.

It was about then, in graduate school, that I started my own personal therapy. I entered treatment because I was separating from my parents who were, at that point, in emotional and financial straits; I was greatly distressed at the concurrence of my need to get away and their other emerging difficulties. How could I go ahead with my life if theirs were falling apart? I had moved three thousand miles away to go to graduate school, to be able to establish my own identity.

MY CHILDHOOD

Over time, I began to realize that my blind spots in the treatment of traumatized patients were related to my own childhood.

My story is in part the story of the immigrant family leaving oppression in hopes of a better life. I had a domineering older brother, two younger sisters, and a much younger brother. My parents both grew up in very poor Jewish immigrant families. Their parents, who spoke Yiddish with some broken English, had escaped the persecution, deprivation, and trauma of the Eastern European ghettos. One of my grandfathers described pogroms, where family members were killed in front of him by Cossacks. Both my parents grew up with deprivation and depression. There was no sexual abuse in the family history, as far as I am aware.

Both my parents described childhoods filled with maltreatment, but they thought of their parents as good and right. Much of the maltreatment that they experienced seemed to be a result of trying to cope with dire circumstances. My parents' idealization of their parents is a common response to trauma, and usually leads to repetition in the next generation because the parental maltreatment is not thought of as maltreatment.

Only with my first therapist could I fully remember, and tell with detail and feeling, my father's violence. My father had been, among many things, a professional boxer. When upset, he was capable of violence. He would discipline me and my siblings by using physical and excessive force. This was accepted by some adults as an appropriate way to treat children. Other aspects of the violence were not in any way related to discipline. When angry at my mother, my father sometimes attacked the children, by kicking them up the stairs or knocking them unconscious with his fist. I usually hid and tried to melt into the walls as a child. During most of these early years, I would leave any room that my father entered if I could. During some of these violent experiences I thought that I or others might die. Early on, I came to the realization that the way out is to understand these people and manage them, or run and hide.

At the beginning of my therapy, I thought of my mother as an empathic and understanding person who was there for me. She had low self-esteem, but was extremely bright and competent. At the same time, she had learning disabilities. She became an R.N. and graduated first in her class at a time when no other family member had ever gone on to higher education. Only after exploring my feelings in therapy did I begin to realize that my mother was not a saint. She could be warm and attentive, but was also angry much of the time. She was also violent with her children. Her behavior was unpredictable. I saw her break a wooden spoon over my brother's head when he was 5. One occurrence stands out in my mind: when I was about 5 years old, my mother was feeding breakfast to my siblings and me. I accidentally knocked over my milk. She started shaking and pinching me until I bled. Later, as an adult, I put together what I thought might be behind this rage attack. When my mother was a child, she was responsible for taking care of her baby sister. Many times, she did not have milk to feed this starving baby sister when their mother went off to work. This was one of many attacks of her rage.

THE IMPACT OF TREATMENT ON THE THERAPIST

Following this personal exploration made possible by my own treatment, I began to hear and be aware of my patients' trauma. I then had additional experiences that evidenced the role of sexual abuse in the etiology of a number of patient difficulties.

At one time I ran several residential programs at a community mental health center for heroin-addicted women, some of whom were pregnant. I facilitated a women's group, and of the twenty women in this group, almost every one reported that she had been sexually molested in childhood. I believe that this abuse contributed heavily to the drug and alcohol problems of these women. They told of shocking experiences such as being sold by their addicted parents to other adults for sex in payment for drugs, or being forced to have sex with dogs and other animals.

This facility was a residential treatment center for men, women, and heroin-addicted pregnant women. I worked with ex-addict staff and addict patients, many of whom had backgrounds of abuse, which they acted out with each other and in their behavior toward me. This was a powerfully moving but stressful job. For the first time in my life I got high blood pressure, which stopped when I quit.

My next job was at a county mental health clinic for children, where I worked for three years. Most of these children were physically abused, and many were sexually abused. Many of them were given labels such as "attention deficit disorder" or "conduct disorder" and treated with medication. In this county facility, a child became a patient if he or she had three treatment failures, or if the parents were trying to abandon the child. Usually, county utilization control would allow only one or possibly two sessions per week to treat a family with multiple suicidal members, no resources, and severe trauma.

I had the following dream during my time at this clinic. It reveals my feelings about working with deprived and traumatized families: My office floods with water and I am trying to climb out before the water gets to the electric wires and seeps through the insulation and electrocutes me.

I began to find that sexual abuse was common among my patients, both male and female. My graduate training was primarily in short-term behavioral and family-systems approaches. Treating sexual abuse and trauma victims more frequently and over a longer period of time was a step up in intensity and a challenge, especially in terms of managing my own feelings. After my three years at the county mental health clinic for children, I moved into private practice. I yearned to treat people more effectively by seeing them more frequently and continuing treatment for the long term. The following is a composite of some of the first such patients I saw.

In my private practice, I first began treating adult survivors of childhood incest multiple times per week in individual therapy. These patients confronted me with a whirlwind of emotions that I could not manage. This was after I had started my own analysis, which exposed more of my own emotions. A patient, a woman in her forties, spoke of her abusive relationships, and I wanted to save her. I wanted to save her as I wished someone had saved me. I tried to convince her to leave these relationships. She turned her love and needs to me, and I felt overwhelmed. She wanted me to show her how to be in a loving sexual relationship. I did not know what to do. I felt defenseless. She sensed what I was feeling immediately. She told me that she needed to know I cared, and that I had to show her my care concretely. I was in a dilemma. Was I damaging her by not giving her more concrete demonstrations of my caring?

At times I wanted to be her knight in shining armor and save her. This was a way of not feeling the helplessness of listening to her traumatic life. I was also aware of the guilt induced in me for what she described as my depriving her. I felt afraid and overwhelmed because I was in a process I could not manage.

Looking back, however, I realize that I was pressured by this patient. Her style of relating felt familiar to me: I experienced her as my demanding mother. I unconsciously connected and related to her in the compliant ways that characterized my childhood relationship with my mother. But back then I was only aware of the guilt for what she let me know was my deprivation of her.

In this case I was enacting rescue fantasies and avoiding her pain because of two related issues. First, her tales of abuse triggered my experience of abuse. Once that happened, I could not tolerate letting the process continue because I felt too much of my own anxiety. Second, I could not maintain my faith in the therapeutic process: it felt too slow in bringing both of us relief.

My patient kept telling me how wonderful I was. I kept telling her I was not. The pressure to be wonderful felt too much for me and too discrepant from my own view of myself. I also felt like I would have to live up to standards that were too high, and I would have to agree to meet her demands.

In my analysis, I began to explore what was motivating my difficulty in listening to my patient's trauma and pain. The following illustrates what I found:

As I listened to my patient's descriptions of abuse, I began to feel overwhelmed. I wondered what was triggering this feeling. I let my mind wander as a way to explore my feelings, and had the following memory from my childhood.

I was probably 3 and my older brother 6 when I watched my father kick him up the stairs. It was shocking to see my big brother kicked repeatedly. Hearing him shriek horrified me. Though afraid he would die, I felt frozen. I was profoundly ashamed for not flinging myself at my father to save my brother, whom I loved so much.

I still feel this shame and guilt. My motivation in being a therapist is in part the need to repair that moment, and other moments, by saving my patients. Listening to this patient's material began to feel like watching my brother being beaten.

My analyst (I had changed from therapy to analysis four times per week) encouraged me to get into supervision, which I did. My supervisor taught me to interpret the patient's underlying need and not to try so hard to meet the concretized demand. He helped me see the transference, and that it wasn't fully me the patient was responding to. I learned about repetition compulsion and reenactment and how they differ from the patient's concrete needs for the therapist to do things. The patient's need to idealize the therapist as a way to gain strength and hope was explained to me. It was not for me to stop the patient's expression of these idealizations at the start of treatment. I absorbed these lessons over a number of years. I was learning to contain both my own and the patient's reactions within the treatment. My success encouraged me to enter an analytic institute to learn more about these processes.

I applied to a psychoanalytic institute, which had not previously been open to psychologists. In the application process there were a number of interviews and essays. Some focused on my personal history and psychological functioning. In these interviews I felt I had to hide the extent of the abuse I sustained as a child, lest I appear too damaged to be admitted. Even now, I do not know whether the situation itself or my shame accounted for my hiding my mother's abuse of me.

At the institute, I learned about transference, repetition compulsion, and similar processes. This was a wonderful experience. In the area of treating sexual abuse, however, my experience at the institute was disillusioning. Some of the senior faculty disavowed the widespread existence of sexual abuse. One senior analyst said, "I've been in practice over forty years and never saw a single sexually abused patient."

When I presented treatment cases of sexual abuse at the institute, I was often challenged and questioned about the reality of the reported abuse. I was told that it could all be fantasy. One analyst told me, "This is not analysis and these patients are not analyzable." Other senior analysts saw the treatment of sexually abused patients as out-side the realm of psychoanalysis, even though Freud treated many incest and sexual-abuse patients. My anger and disillusionment at this disavowal motivated me to publish four articles on the psychoana-lytic treatment of sexual abuse; it is one of the underlying motives in writing this book. This anger fit one of the motives for this book—to break a childhood dynamic that I was not supposed to tell any-one about the family abuse.

In my private practice, I found that I was often the fourth or fifth therapist whom my patients had seen. In some cases the previous therapist laid the foundation upon which my work with the patient could go deeper. Some other therapists seemed to give the patient the message that the therapist was not open to exploring or listen-ing to the details of the trauma, or even more strongly that it was the fantasy of the patient.

I wondered if I had a bias that encouraged me to see abuse where it did not exist. After exploring this with my patients, supervisors, and peers, I do not believe that this is the situation. The material emerges even when I do not bring it up or raise questions about it. In many cases there was confirmation from objective evidence and from family members.

As I became more convinced of the reality of sexual abuse of chil-dren, I began to present my ideas more openly by teaching, writing, and speaking about them. Then the California state legislature passed a law requiring training in detection and treatment of child abuse for renewal of mental health licenses. I felt supported by the social system at last. I prepared to teach such a course, and taught work-shops on abused children, with a heavy emphasis on sexual abuse detection and treatment. In my article, "Unlocking Incest Memories: Preoedipal Transference, Countertransference, and the Body" (Perlman 1993), I emphasized the prevalent tendency among sexual abuse patients to speak through their bodies. I emphasized that physi-cal sensations are a mode in which traumatic memories are commu-nicated. When one establishes a secure and safe relationship, body memories emerge. This is illustrated in the treatment of Celeste, a second patient I will follow through this book.

Celeste had many operations, including a hysterectomy, in an attempt to treat her extreme pain. But the pain persisted even after the operations. Upon later exploration in analysis, we discovered that she experienced her memories of sexual abuse as pain in her genitals. I believe that much of what we treat as chronic pain in patients actually involves memories of trauma encoded as kinesthetic "body memories." I felt horrified that doctors had performed these surgeries without considering psychological causes. There was an almost-magical transformation of this patient's life as the body manifestations opened up into direct memories of trauma and incest.

At the time that I was treating Celeste, I remembered an experience I had had with my father on the telephone a number of years earlier. I was in the process of telling him how I was, and I told him I had been having migraines for months. He said, "You don't have headaches. You have stomach problems like me."

Right there on the phone I stopped having a headache and started having "stomach problems." I never had a migraine again, but at times still have "stomach problems." Even though I was an adult, the power of my abusive father and my fears that he might kill me were still compelling. Using these personal associations helped me understand what occurred with my patients.

Sexually abused and traumatized patients are frequently symbolically communicating memories of abuse. The abuse is communicated in the words and metaphors they use, their postures, the sensations in their bodies, their dreams and repetitive patterns of living, and in rituals and relationships.

One patient came into my office and complained that her minister kept "poking" her; she was referring to his verbal remarks. She used the word three more times in describing this. I asked, "You use this word *poking* often. What comes to mind about poking?" She said, "A penis." She was surprised at her own response. I asked, "What came to mind about a penis poking you?" This question eventually led to her memory of being raped as a child. What affected me was how easily this memory emerged when she was asked directly, in a safe environment. Although this was not her first therapy experience, she had never before discussed the issue.

HOW WORKING WITH TRAUMA TRIGGERED MY OWN TRAUMA

In my personal analysis, I explored the memories of two accidents that I had been involved in as a child. This helped me develop the concept of body memories. The affects associated with my early memories were sometimes accompanied by flashbacks or images.

I had two life-threatening traffic accidents in my early adolescence that were traumatic in themselves, but also interfered with my healthy separation from my mother. Prior to therapy, if I had been asked point blank about these events, I would have been intellectually aware of the specific details of what happened, but cut off from their emotional impact. Even though I was regularly having recurrent nightmares about the accidents and experiencing their impact on my body, I remained unaware of their extensive meaning and continuing effects on my life until I explored them in therapy. It is important to realize that the impact of traumatic events is encoded in the context of the interpersonal relationships. This is illustrated by my experiences of these accidents. Also, these memories were repeatedly triggered by material I heard from my patients. In my analysis, I realized how often I used the words *smack* and *smack it.*

The first accident occurred when I was 10. My mother had always been a very dominating figure. I found a mouse caught in a mousetrap we had set in the kitchen. I showed my mother the mouse, and she screamed in fear. I chased her all around the house, then hopped on my bike and started riding to the bike store. I was hit by a car. Smack! I remember every detail of the impact and the other cars almost hitting me and swerving while I lay in the street. I was taken to the hospital by ambulance and had surgery. I had to stay in the hospital for months, and was in a body cast for many more. I think I encoded this experience as: "If I challenge my mother she will kill me for sure." This was my worldview from previous family violence, and I assimilated the accident into the template. During the recovery period, my mother was ever-present and attentive to my needs. I was once again totally dependent on her, which I think she liked. Even though I had a sense of conflict about my dependence on her, I was grateful for her attentiveness. I received individual home schooling in secular and religious studies. With this individual attention, I learned how to learn and to study and compensate for my previous learning difficulties.

The second traffic accident occurred when I was 12 years old. I went on a bus trip with the junior high school band. This was the first major trip I took away from my family. I was sitting in the front seat with my friends. It was a long trip and I wanted to take a nap, so I switched seats with a friend in the back of the bus. A short time later, the bus driver fell asleep and the bus **crashed**. At first all I was aware of was the impact of my body hitting the seat in front of me. I looked up and there was glass flying and people yelling all around. I crawled out of the broken glass and bent metal of the bus and sat on a rock. I looked back at the scene of devastation. I lost my ability to see for hours.

The boy who sat in my seat and two others, all friends of mine, were killed. I was in the hospital for a few hours, after which I was taken home by my father. Although I was taken care of physically, no one ever asked me how I felt or what I thought. As far as I could remember, I did not attend any funerals. I went to school for five more years with many of the same kids who had been on the bus. No one ever made reference to the accident.

In my initial therapies, I and my therapists tended to attribute all the fear and trauma of my childhood to my parents, and, to a lesser extent, to my brother. After ten years of treatment with four therapists, I began to recognize the impact of the traffic accidents. I began to talk about my feelings regarding the bus accident and my guilt for switching seats. I reexperienced the trauma in the sessions, with complete recall. This took place with a soothing peripheral awareness of my analyst's quiet presence. During my analysis I realized I would have a recurrent dream each time something positive would happen in my life: The boy who had died in my seat would come, maggot-ridden and decomposed, and try to grab me. I would try to run but he would grab my shoulder. I would wake up in terror.

I think that I tried not to enjoy good things or successes as a way of trying not to have this punishing dream.

Often, I would begin to reexperience the accident in which I was hit by a car when I attempted to confront an authority figure or a maternal figure. It is as if that accident were punishment for my having challenged my mother. Any sight of blood or hospitals would result in my reexperiencing both accidents. Details of my patients' traumas also were sufficient, at times, to trigger the retraumatization.

Many times I would feel toward my patients as I would toward my siblings: responsible and guilty for their pain at the hands of my mother and father. My relationships with my siblings were neglected by many of my therapists. My older brother was beaten in front of me by both parents, and then he would beat me. I tried to teach my next younger sister to hide, but she tried to stand up to my parents, so she was hit harder and more often than the rest of us. I would advise her, "Just say 'Yes, sir' and leave the room." The abuse of my brother and sister stands out to me as more terrible, painful, and guilt-producing than my own abuse. I had learned to hide, or go numb if hit.

My role as a therapist was also shaped by my childhood experiences. I became my mother's therapist as a child to survive her. Listening to her upset and pain was a way of stabilizing her and then maybe I could feel loved and be attended to. Taking this role also warded off my mother's self-absorbed rejection of my needs, and my awareness of my own needs by deferring to her needs. It also helped me avoid my father's wrath. When my parents would fight, my father later might say to me, "Talk to your mother." I would do what he said immediately. I would be safe during the explosive aggression by complying with my father's demands and also by helping to stabilize the chaotic and violent family crisis. This represented the beginnings of my therapist role in the family, which allowed me some sense of value and importance. This dynamic is discussed by Alice Miller (1981) in her book *The Drama of the Gifted Child.*

Cultural issues have been critical to my experience of being a therapist. Sacrifice and guilt are prominent themes in Jewish culture. My mother, as a good Jewish mother does, used to tell me how she carried me in her stomach for nine months, and my father would tell about how he sacrificed all pleasure and happiness for his family. Guilt, especially survivor guilt, is a Jewish tradition. My grandfather told me of his experiences with pogroms in Russia, and my mother gave me many books to read about the Holocaust as soon as I was able to read. I fasted for my sins each year on the High Holidays, and prayed, "Please God, for-give me for the sins I have committed!" It is ambiguous to what extent my motivations to sacrifice and care for others, and to feel responsibil-ity and guilt for others' pain, are the legacies of the Jewish culture in which I grew up (cultural trauma), and/or the product of accidents I de-scribed above, and my traumatic personal experience of them, and the traumatic inattention with which these experiences were met. I wonder how much this encoding of my life experience arose out of my personal experience, and how much of it was an intergenerational transmission of trauma in a culture filled with guilt.

Like other therapists with similar backgrounds, I have had to be vigi-lant not to assume that I know what a patient's experience is, because I may be organizing their experience through my own experience. This has been a process of learning to sit and listen, to contain the impulse to intervene. This impulse is usually a way of moving away from my own pain.

CHAPTER 5

Therapist Rescue Fantasies

Many people who become psychoanalysts have in their childhood histories a common element of having been required unduly to serve archaic selfobject functions for a parent (Miller 1979), a requirement that is readily revived in reaction to patients' archaic states and developmental longings. When empathy is equated with an ideal of optimal human responsiveness and at the same time rightfully claimed to lie at the heart of the psychoanalytic process, this can exacerbate the analyst's countertransference dilemma, which takes the form of a requirement to provide the patient with an unbroken selfobject experience uncontaminated by painful repetitions of past childhood traumata—a requirement now invoked in the name of Kohut, Bacal, or Stolorow. As Brandchaft (1988) observes, when an analyst comes under the grip of such a requirement, the quintessential psychoanalytic aim of investigating and illuminating the patient's inner experience can become significantly subverted. [Stolorow 1994, p. 44]

Therapist rescue fantasies are one of the most frequent issues that derail the treatment of sexually abused and traumatized patients. These rescue fantasies are usually related to the depth of feeling that is triggered inside the therapist in response to seeing the pain of his or her patients. This can commonly cause the therapist to feel helpless in the face of wishing to help the patient in pain, as well as triggering similar experiences of helplessness in the therapist's own history. Adding more fuel to this situation is the mixture of the therapist's own dynamics, the dynamics of traumatized patients, and a context of social controversy.

Alice Miller (1981), in her book *The Drama of the Gifted Child*, outlines a typical therapist's childhood. Often this childhood involves repeated efforts to meet the parents' narcissistic needs. The child feels totally dependent on the parent and must comply with their needs. This sets the stage for children learning to take a caregiver role. This drama is enacted throughout the therapist's life, particularly with patients. The therapist's patients come to represent the parents whose needs emotionally compel the child's deference and yet can never be satisfied.

A related common dynamic for therapists involves a search to repair the deprivations and traumas of their own lives by curing patients, who are seen as representing the therapists' needy child parts. This is done in part by the therapist simulating what the therapist longed for and needed but never got as a child. The therapist's own transferential motivations for patients synergistically interact with his or her traumatized patients' intense needs and panic; the result may be that the therapist's dramas (the futile effort to satisfy the narcissistic needs of the caregiver) are repeatedly reenacted to the point of emotional exhaustion.

In their childhood many therapists experienced loss, threatened abandonment, or the death of a loved one or parent. When patients enact a piece of their own trauma, such as the wish or compulsion to commit suicide, therapists may reexperience their own trauma. In these situations, therapists can experience patients as the abandoning and/or sadistic parents.

One therapist, whose mother repeatedly told him she was going to die of a heart attack, and that his demands exacerbated this, was vulnerable to his patients' threats of suicide. The therapist reexperienced the childhood fears of losing his mother and being the cause of her death in the moment when the patient made these threats. This reduced his functioning as a therapist at these moments.

Another therapist whose mother died in his childhood spent his life taking care of patients. In this way, he unconsciously searched for his lost mother and the caregiving he missed. He often overextended himself trying to save patients.

The social controversy surrounding treatment of abused and traumatized patients adversely reduces professional and personal support for patients and therapists. In the wake of the false-memory controversy, therapists have been accused of manufacturing patients' memories. These accusations can further enmesh the patient and therapist, who may feel isolated and attacked. (This issue is discussed in detail in Chapter 16.) In these dynamics, therapists can become overinvolved with protecting and advocating for patients, and then be more vulnerable to patients' threats of suicide or abandonment. Disentangling these overidentifications with patients is a step in making the treatment more manageable.

Treating these patients is a humbling experience; as therapists, we have to accept our human limitations. I have had to come to terms with my rescue fantasies, and to accept that I cannot save all these patients, just as I could not save my siblings and parents.

As an undergraduate I volunteered in the middle boys' ward at Kings Park State Hospital in New York. I felt profoundly sad each time I visited these abandoned, abused, disturbed boys. I wanted to take home several boys whom I had started to care about. When I realized the impracticality of these fantasies, I felt I had to stop going to the ward. It was too painful to see the effects of the destruction they had suffered and lack of help in the present. I was able to continue only by deciding that I would focus not on how terrible their lives were, but on the benefits of my help, and on the belief that my concern was my gift to them.

This basic adaptation worked until I began doing long-term deeper therapy, when I was forced to face more of the patients' pain. As I got deeper into this, my rescue and adoption fantasies increased, as did my difficulties in setting limits. Looking back, I recognize that my survivor guilt interfered with clear-headed and effective work.

Dealing with patients' enactments of their childhood abuse, trauma, self-hate, death wishes, fragmented selves, and threats of suicide can be extremely frightening. Dealing with suicide threats can trigger many experiences from the therapists' own past, including intense feelings of helplessness. Therapists may have difficulty setting appropriate limits because they fear patient suicides. Below are some dreams I had while working with some chronically suicidal patients. These illustrate the fear of setting limits during late-night suicidal phone calls.

> I was working in a mental hospital and said "No!" to a patient. Then I see the cliff from which the patient committed suicide. I see the blood on the rocks below. I had been so proud of myself for saying "No."

> How dare I take a day off and have a good time, when my suicidal patient is working so hard?

Finally after a number of nights with disrupted sleep because of these nightmares, I had the following dream: I don't want to dream, because I'm afraid of dreaming.

My internal dialogue that opens the Introduction of this book illustrates the intrapsychic work I had to do, to be able to set more appropriate limits without feeling bad or experiencing intense self-recrimination. What I needed to do was differentiate myself from my family and their painful dramas, differentiate my patient from my family of origin, and accept my limited ability to affect another person's life. I needed to accept that the person I was trying to help was the one who had to make the changes. At best I could remain open, point the way, and give encouragement. Realizing this felt like letting the air out of my inflated fantasy of being an all-powerful therapist.

As I have come to feel more comfortable with setting limits, I came to see helping patients as having potential pitfalls as well as benefits. I needed to be careful not to reinforce the patients' view of themselves as helpless and as victims. It has become apparent that sometimes providing patients with lowered fees and extra phone calls, and allowing them to run up a debt, because of their entitled feeling that the trauma has hurt them and they should not have to have more pain in their lives, can encourage enactments of mistreating the therapist as well as not helping the patient live in a new effective way in the world. Each request needs to be explored and used as clinically necessary.

> A critical set of interactions occurred around Ann's not paying her bill. On exploring this, what emerged was that she felt the world owed her for the trauma she had suffered; not only her parents but everyone, including me, would have to make good on this debt. She therefore felt justified in not paying her bill. She expressed much anger over my insistence that she pay. To be able to pay, she would have to find employment. We explored these issues but this did not change her behavior. After my telling her she had to pay her current bill each month or I would have to reduce the frequency of her sessions, Ann applied herself to a job search and, within weeks, found employment. She expressed great pride in her ability to better her financial situation. Upon exploring she said she was somewhat surprised to learn that I had needs, and that what I wanted was a reasonable fee and not a sexual relationship with her.

Managing to set limits and stay in role is critical. The patient's needs come in contact with the therapist's limitations regularly. These limitations will usually result in the patient learning that his or her hope for the therapist to directly satisfy most of his or her needs will not be fulfilled. For example, patients are expected to pay their bill. The patient will need to realize that therapists have only so much energy and time to attend to them, other patients, professional activities, family, and friends.

It is critical how this issue is handled. I try to tell patients what I can and cannot do based on my limitations. This focuses attention on my limitations, rather than their needs, reducing their perceived "badness."

To maintain perspective, I try to view the needs of the patient in the context of being in a long-term relationship. The goal is to design a relationship that works for both participants. Naturally, in this profession the design needs to leave room for creative solutions. Some overextension by the therapist may be required and tolerated for short periods; but if it goes on too long it can engender the therapist's resentment, which in turn can interfere with the safety and ambiance of the patient–therapist relationship. Without commenting on it at the time to the patient, it is very important to model self-regulation and limit-setting for them.

The issue of setting limits has to be balanced with the need for the therapist to be there for the patient, sometimes in very concrete ways. Many of these patients are too fearful to take care of necessities. The therapist may choose to take an advocacy role or pragmatic coaching stance. For example, patients may need help budgeting their money or filling out an application for a job. The therapist can participate in the session in helping the patient complete these tasks.

For example, in the midst of intense crisis, the patient may require more contact with the therapist than usual. This can be arranged in a way that balances the needs of the patient and the comfort level of the therapist. First I try to understand and explore what process the patient is experiencing that results in the requests for connection. This need usually has some specific meaning related to the "openings" discussed in this book (e.g., needing to feel heard, or important, or needing to combat the feeling of being "bad"). Based on this exploration, strategies for managing the patient's needs are developed. But the individual tolerances of therapists and patients are important to be considered. Some therapists are comfortable with late-night calls, others are not. I am not. I tell the patient I need my sleep or else I cannot be effective as their therapist on an ongoing basis. This is my need; it does not imply that the patient is "bad." I tell the patient what I am willing to do. For example, I try using transitional objects to reduce the demands for late-night contact. I am willing to make tapes of my reading them stories or of my saying soothing things, or give them concrete transitional objects that help them hold on to their connection to me.

CHAPTER 6

Therapy Openings

In this book the descriptions of the therapist's history have tended to be traumatic in nature. This may imply to the reader that for a therapist to be effective with these patients, he or she must have a similar traumatic background. In my experience of supervising many therapists, I have found that the key element in therapist effectiveness is the therapists' openness to empathically immerse themselves in the patient's experience and not the therapists' histories of trauma. That is why openness and openings are discussed in detail.

Openings are emotional states of readiness to take in and experience deeply, and to be real and connected. This readiness is profoundly shaped by the person's assumptions about what exists and how things work; assumptions that influence perceptions and behavior. At moments, people can transcend their assumptions. It takes willingness and strength to face ambiguity and anxiety. These challenges arise for both patient and therapist.

There can be openings within a person to parts of themselves; this is sometimes called "being more in touch with oneself." There are also openings to the experience of others, called empathy. In treatment, to open the door to deeper experience, there must be a connection between the patient and therapist. Over and over again, patients will ask the therapist to demonstrate the ability to create and contain the process, so that they can develop faith in a new experience and trust in the process. Each time the therapist helps create an opening and navigate through it, the process can deepen, and healing can proceed. It deepens in the sense that patients begin to believe more fully that they can tell the therapist their feelings and thoughts, and have them accepted without ridicule or attack. The therapist's ability to hear, see, and respond to patients as patients see themselves, rather than seeing them through a web of assumptions and projections, facilitates the patients' feeling safe enough to reveal more of their experience. Then patients bring the therapist into their hidden world, a world that contains many experiences they had been too afraid to tell to others. These may be dark, shattering experiences that patients are frightened to look at, or experiences of psychological starvation that were not understood and have not been integrated into their life.

This issue of access to experience in patients is complex. Patients may be aware of only parts of experience, or they may not be conscious of the traumatic experiences and their implications because they are too threatening.

To deepen the process of treatment, it is necessary for patients to access different types of memory and emotion. This requires the building of trust about their ability to live through the process, as these memories are experienced. The therapist must work to build mutual trust and a history with the patient, so that both can see that the process works, and both can be trusted to play their part responsibly.

The therapist's development of trust in the patient's ability to be responsive to the therapist's emotional needs is also important. This responsiveness allows the therapist to function at deeper levels.

> Ann had given me a gift of a fan to look at when I was upset by the disclosure of the graphic details of her traumas. Her gift illustrated that she was accurately aware of my difficulties observing her revelations. If she had criticized me at that moment, I might have become defensive and denied my difficulties. That would have set the treatment back

and caused a rupture in our mutual trust. Instead, she gave me a concrete interpretation of my difficulty, together with a gift. There was no direct verbal statement of my difficulties that day by me or the patient. The focus of our work was on her art and her feelings about me, not on my reactions. Her gift of the fan and her discussion of her coping strategies was a well-timed piece of therapeutic work, which enabled me to continue to help her. It is only in hindsight that I can appreciate what occurred. But even at the time, I was aware that she was helping me with my difficulties self-regulating while taking in the horror of her story, and I appreciated it. A few days later we explored her experience and I acknowledged her help and thanked her.

My acknowledgment of her help was crucial to her. Since her childhood, she had been trained to care for others, especially her parents, but had never received credit for these special talents. In childhood she did this out of fear and need of deep attachment, and she did the same with me.

Sometimes when the therapist responds in the hoped-for way and helps to open the door, patients become frightened, because it unhinges them from their set expectations; it disrupts the comfort and security that they have struggled to achieve. Then patients are faced with opening up and letting the therapist into their world. This is seen as a terrible risk by many patients. For if hopes are raised and then disappointed, it may be unbearable. Other patients refuse to come close because they love the therapist so much, and assume it was their own badness that caused the abuse in the first place; they protect the loved therapist by not moving forward in the treatment.

If the therapist repeatedly ignores or punishes these openings, the stakes may be raised and demands can escalate. Patients may create another version of the test of the doorway: Some patients or therapists protest, and pound on the locked doors. Some give up in pain and resignation. Repeated failure of these tests can create a negative spiral, destroying the treatment and ultimately the patient's hope. Without hope many patients cannot go on. Sensing this, the therapist may feel desperate or completely detached, and denigrate the patient.

PART II

OPENINGS TO TRAUMA AND PAIN

Part II, "Openings to Trauma and Pain," presents a conceptualization of the therapeutic process as it changes over the course of treatment. I have found this conceptualization useful in guiding my work and communicating the process to others. The chapters discuss the general stages and developmental tasks that therapists and patients navigate in the healing process. Each task is constellated around an opening (in the sense of readiness to take and allow in another's deeper experience) to healing that the patient and therapist need to struggle through together. For the therapist this process may be called empathic immersion in the patient's experience, and for the patient this process may be called trusting and opening up to the therapist. Which opening, question, or task takes foreground and which takes background are determined by the interactive needs of both participants. Each question is addressed in a chapter in the book. The treatment process is divided into two stages, characterized by a series of questions or openings.

I discuss the course of treatment as it usually develops for traumatized and abused patients. After considering some basic assumptions of my approach to treating abused and traumatized patients, I review two other authors' models of treatment with these patients that have influenced my work, and then present my own.

BASIC ASSUMPTIONS

Basic to my framework of understanding is that child abuse and related trauma have pervasive and formative effects on human development, and that the traumatized person, their families, and society often avoid acknowledging these effects because they are painful. To help patients face their traumas, therapists may be required to acknowledge their own traumatic experiences and pain, as well as the pain they themselves may have inflicted on others.

This framework is primarily based on a relational model of motivation. It assumes that human connection and attachment, love, and a sense of belonging are central motivating forces in human behavior. My formulation of the questions posed at each treatment stage is also influenced by a humanistic and a self-psychological view of human growth. One of the basic premises of humanistic psychology is that people have an innate desire to grow and develop to their fullest. Maslow (1962), a pioneer of this approach, called this the desire for "self-actualization." Embedded in this framework are some aspects of Maslow's hierarchy of needs. In this hierarchy, safety and bodily needs must be met before other emotional needs can be taken up. Both self psychology and humanistic psychology emphasize how disruption and trauma can split the self. Ferenczi (1933) emphasized that there can be no trauma without some splitting of the psyche. Self psychology (Shane et al. 1997) emphasizes how the experience of being understood and of having a new relationship is central to healing.

Treatment is conceptualized as a relationship context for the patient that offers empathy and support with which the patient can reintegrate and work through the patient's traumatic experiences. As Alice Miller (1981, 1983, 1984, 1988) states, if the abused and traumatized person/child is given a supportive and empathic environment within which to work out the trauma, the likelihood of pathology is reduced.

TWO INFLUENTIAL THEORISTS

Herman (1992), in her book *Trauma and Recovery*, sets out a three-stage model of treatment for short-term survivor group therapy. In the first stage the patient's safety issues are dealt with, including real-life current dangers, fears of the trauma recurring, and trust issues for the patient with the therapist. In the second stage the patient needs to reconstruct the trauma and explore its meaning. In the third stage the patient needs to be helped to reconnect to other people and acquire a sense of belonging, which had been disrupted by the trauma. Herman sees as one of the central treatment goals to connect or reconnect the patient to the therapist, significant others, the community, and, possibly, to a religious faith. Although this book presents a two-stage treatment model, it was influenced by the usefulness of Herman's articulation of her clinical methodology in terms of a sequence of stages. Additionally, the clinical contents and treatment objectives of each of Herman's three stages are acknowledged as sound and addressed in the book's model.

Davies and Frawley (1992a, 1994) have a relational model of treatment with a transference–countertransference paradigm. Here they view the patient and therapist as involved in interlocking reenactments. Davies and Frawley (1994) describe their eight scripts as follows:

> We have found that there are eight relational positions, expressed within four relational matrices, alternately enacted by therapist and survivor in the transference and countertransference, that repeatedly recur in psychoanalytic work with adult survivors of childhood sexual abuse. These include the uninvolved nonabusing parent and the neglected child; the sadistic abuser and the helpless, impotently enraged victim; the idealized, omnipotent rescuer and the entitled child who demands to be rescued; and the seducer and the seduced. Although these, of course, do not account for every aspect of the transference and countertransference with every patient, our experience is that these eight positions and four matrices are enacted with sufficient regularity that a thorough familiarity with their clinical manifestations is invaluable to the analytic work. [p. 167]

Many themes that are delineated in these eight relational positions within four sets of interlocking dramas are also embedded in the questions, issues, and openings in my book. Davies and Frawley's relational positions are fixed positions involving two persons, usually involving central critical issues. This book describes these fixed positions in terms of the central issues between two people. This allows more variety as to how each therapist–patient pair articulates its needs in relation to the issues and to each other. Many important dynamics are not covered by Davies and Frawley's set relational positions. For example, in my experience, sibling and grandparent transferences can be as powerful as the dynamics listed by Davies and Frawley. In my internal dialogue at the start of the Introduction, I illustrated the power of watching my sister being abused and the centrality of this in my enactment of being a therapist.

Based on my experience of treating and supervising the treatment of many sexually abused and traumatized patients, I have distilled basic questions that these patients bring to treatment within each of these two stages of treatment. The questions can also be thought of as developmental tasks the therapeutic couple needs to negotiate together. I have highlighted some of the underlying influences and assumptions behind the questions. I will delineate the common patterns, but there are critical differences that always exist in treatment; one must bear in mind that each person, with his or her personal history and subjective experience, is ultimately unique, as is each patient–therapist pair.

Understanding the central emotional questions and openings presented by abused patients, and the most frequent emotional reactions and responses of therapists, prepares the therapist to engage in successful treatment. These questions are conceptualized in a way that humanizes the needs of the patient, so as to increase the therapist's empathy. They are also stated in a manner that attempts to normalize the patient's needs, in order to reduce his or her sense of shame and humiliation.

First Stage of Treatment: Establishing Safety and Connection

The basis of stages in my model is that certain issues of safety, emotional containment, and feeling heard (validation through mirroring) need to be dealt with initially for a successful treatment process to be set on course. These patients are usually asking in many ways, "Can I exist and live a life?" Successfully working through some layers of these issues helps mobilize a positive and containing maternal transference, which is necessary for a constructive deeper process. Here the patient needs a deep, close experience of the therapist as a good containing other, and even a sense of positive merger or connection. In traditional analytic literature this transference has been called a "preoedipal transference." In self psychology it has been referred to as a "selfobject," "merger," "idealizing," or "mirroring" transference. The issues that need to be navigated for the deep maternal transference to be activated can vary, given the patient–therapist pair.

Once the first stage is in place, the second stage of treatment can occur. No issue that emerges in the first or second stage ever fully disappears, but it may recede to the background of the therapy experience. Other critical issues can emerge in the foreground, determined by the specific needs and experiences of the unique intersubjective pair of patient and therapist. Salient questions or issues shift and are constantly revisited. These issues are constellated around openings to deeper experience.

Signs that the early maternal transference is in place are discussed in more detail in Chapter 11. Described briefly, the therapist watches for signs that the patient looks forward to sessions, longing to be there with the loved therapist and feeling happy to be in the therapist's presence. Young feelings of childhood begin to emerge. Hope and fear of a new way of being are expressed.

This stage model is predicated on some basic clinical processes. A recurring concept in this book is that the earlier and more severe the trauma, the greater the demand to forget, the less the emotional support for the victim, and thus the greater the likelihood that the trauma will be dissociated and split off into the body. Early trauma is primarily encoded in kinesthetic/body memories. These early experiences predate the stable use of language; their access through the use of verbal therapies is limited. These early memories, as well as overwhelming traumatic memories that occur at an older age, are dissociated so that they are experienced as automatic, procedural (body) memory, and are not integrated into the narrative of the victim's experience. The body, as a result, is often an important source or opening into these traumatic experiences, whereas a focus on words in psychotherapy may not reveal the existence of these experiences.

Mobilization of a successful maternal transference sets in motion the reliving of the childhood and/or adult trauma paired with the positive experience of the therapist, a process that enables the patient to reintegrate the memories. By helping the patient to feel safe and protected in therapy, the therapist facilitates the patient's recollection and exploration of the abuse or trauma, which would be too frightening to do alone. Painful body sensations can then be transformed into concrete memories of abuse relived with the affects, sensations, and images integrated. This results in the reduction of pain, increased aliveness, and greater coherence in the patient's sense of self, now that the levels of experience do not have to be kept separate.

These patients need to be taught to slow down and become aware of their moment-to-moment experience, especially their body experience. This helps them recognize what it is they are actually feeling and reintegrate their own memories. So much of experience for these patients is automatic, such that moment-to-moment decisions are made based on feeling states that may be triggered from the past but are identified as emanating from the current situation. These feeling states may be intolerable and unpleasant such that they are unconsciously and automatically avoided as a way of coping with their present life. Many times the trauma is reexperienced in daily reactions or affective states. Helping patients sit with these affect states allows them time to learn what is controlling their behavior, to explore these affect states, and to learn what they are really about. This enables patients to more fully navigate in the present rather than continuing to be trapped in the past or the flight from the ever-threatening past.

The questions of the first stage usually include the following:

"*Will you hurt, ignore, or help me?*" This question focuses on the patient's fear and need for self-protection. I believe that most people are frightened of opening up to another person. For traumatized patients this is even more exaggerated because the world and other people have betrayed and/or hurt them by action or omission, such that treatment is asking these patients to go against their own experience. If this issue is not successfully managed, no effective treatment can occur.

"*Can I have power over myself?*" This question highlights the importance of helping patients be aware of, and take control over, their own physical and emotional needs (self-regulation). These patients are usually out of touch with their central bodily and emotional functions—for example, many are too fearful or anxious to be able to think clearly. If the therapist tries to talk to a patient who is overwhelmed without first soothing him, the patient will not be able to communicate effectively and may also experience this as a major misattunement.

"*Can you hear me?*" This question pinpoints the patient's need to be heard and acknowledged as a person. These patients have had their feelings and sense of agency ignored. They therefore need this experience of being heard and acknowledged as a central aspect of treatment to enable them to engage in a deep therapeutic process.

These are the questions that, in one form or another, patients are commonly asking in the first stage of the treatment process.

CHAPTER 7

Will You Hurt, Ignore, or Help Me? Fear and Self-Protection

FEAR AND DISCONNECTION

Feelings of danger, fear, and helplessness are intrinsic to the experience of trauma (Herman 1992). Being haunted by and in fear of the traumatic event reoccurring is a hallmark symptom of survivors. According to current psychological and biological theory, the flight-or-fight response to danger is biologically determined. Trauma patients are filled with the terror of annihilation. Their fundamental question is, "Is it safe enough for me to exist?"

Herman (1992) emphasizes a related central effect of trauma on human relationships. In addition to the fear, traumatized patients have a deep conviction that others do not care for them, because others did not protect and help them in their time of greatest need. This compounds the impact of their fear because they feel that not only are they in danger, but no one else will care enough to try to help.

In the first stage of treatment, more concretely, on initial contact patients may ask, "Will you hurt, ignore, or help?" The patients' expectations of the therapist are heavily influenced by their past experiences with authority figures, specifically caregivers. Even in situ-

ations where the trauma was not perpetrated by other people, patients usually held others responsible because, as children, they saw
adults as all-powerful. Also, other people usually have been unwilling
to listen and provide support after the trauma, creating a secondary
traumatization. For many of these patients the fears are complex,
because the source of danger and attack was the natural protector
and provider, the parent or caregiver. This sets up a state of paralysis or fleeing within the patient that I call "dissociation." Children
have fewer psychic defenses than adults; therefore, the earlier and
more violent and stressful the trauma, the greater the dissociation.
These patients have learned to survive by hiding their true selves and
needs. The maneuvers they use to survive the abuse arise automatically in anxiety-provoking situations, including therapy.

This is a difficult set of crosscurrents to manage for the patient
and the therapist. Other needs can become the foreground for a time,
but anything can retrigger the primacy of the fear. Even in this first
opening question of fear there are aspects of future issues or openings, but they are secondary to the fear. My own history has sensitized me to this.

> In my own treatment, as I delved deeper into my pain, I became aware
> of how frightened I was in every aspect of my life. Over my twenty years
> of treatment, at several points I felt less afraid, but I was shocked to
> notice how fearful I still was. Each time I was able to take in only a por-
> tion of the fear I carried. I noticed how sounds scared me, as did people's
> anger, or even the anticipation of anger. Any of these effects could shape
> my behavior drastically. Many things I knew were not really dangerous
> but they nonetheless had the power to frighten me. I realized that each
> time I did something I thought another person might not like, I feared
> that he or she would turn into my violent mother, father, or brother, or
> that I would be hit by a car. This helped me realize the level of fear that
> traumatized patients carry around with them.

On a practical level, the fear and danger experienced by trauma
survivors must always be kept in mind. This needs to be taken in at
a deep level by the therapist. The issue of safety is paramount with
these patients, who often have lives filled with abuse and danger.

They may be living with perpetrators who threaten to kill them for telling, or there may be abusive husbands, exploitative families, or lifestyles filled with serious risks of death.

These threats can come from external sources, but they can also come from within. Suicide is often a real possibility and can raise the therapist's anxiety level. Parts of these patients may want to die, or to kill other parts. The question "Will you help me to survive and be safer?" is immediately concretized, and powerful enactments can occur around it. These dangers can be frightening and can preoccupy the therapist; at other times, the therapist can be in denial about the seriousness of such dangers. Some traumatized survivors do kill themselves.

Still another pattern involves patients who have given up, who feel nothing for others, and are sometimes dangerous. They may feel no compassion or empathy, and can easily use and abuse others. Miller (1984) comments that it only takes one supportive relationship in the formative years of childhood to make the difference between a mass murderer and a person capable of care. Violent abuse occurring in the early years of life and lack of subsequent support can create a profound disconnection from others. Yet there are some children who, by some constitutional ability, are able to survive horrific situations with some sense of self and empathy. Early on, many of these children are able to label the parent as crazy or mean, and thereby not internalize the abuse as much.

Most of these patients desperately want to be attached to others, despite their fear of what can happen in relationships. They may give gifts and compliments to the therapist, because they are trying to stave off anticipated rage. It can be hard for the therapist to accept this idea. It is seductive to believe instead that all of the patient's positive overtures are meant for the therapist at face value and deserved. Therapists as a group tend to find meaning in their lives by helping others and trying to feel worthwhile by experiencing the patient's appreciation and gratitude. They experience the patient's reactions as a mirror in which they can see themselves. When they see terror in their patients' faces, it usually makes them feel that they must be doing something to hurt the patients, and this evokes guilt.

The therapist may react with anger over this, communicating, in essence, "You are wrong for feeling this way about me; other people don't react that way," rather than remaining open and exploring the patient's experience. The self-object needs of the therapist have been recognized only sporadically in the psychoanalytic literature (e.g., Bacal and Thompson 1996, Searles 1975).

FIRST SESSION

These patients' fears and hyperarousal can be contagious and unsettling for the therapist. Therapists may be anxious about meeting a new person with unpredictable demands; they will have their own fears or expectations of others. Usually traumatized and sexually abused patients seek treatment when they are in crisis and their lives are often tumultuous. The patients' traumas are communicated to the therapist through the empathic connection; they are asking, "Can you tolerate my fear and give me permission to talk about my pain?"

Even before the first contact with the therapist, transference is activated. What has this patient been told about the therapist? In what context will the therapy be conducted? In the first phone call the tension between the patient's hope and fear has already begun: "Help! I'm afraid you will hurt me, but I'm also afraid to continue living like this, so I'm desperate enough to reach out right now." The patient is acutely aware of the tonal qualities of the therapist's voice and the implications of the therapist's responses.

Treatment needs a good beginning, or it may end abruptly. Abuse and trauma patients have survived by developing especially sensitive antennae—the ability to detect minute shifts in emotional states. At the same time, the abuse or trauma has often numbed them to their current surroundings. They are still lost in reexperiencing the unprocessed trauma. Cues that one might not expect to be experienced as traumatic are regularly interpreted as forewarnings of disaster or retraumatization, and they frequently expect powerful people to exploit or hurt them. For example, even the therapist's kind behavior may be seen as a cue that the worst is coming, since their childhood abuser may have been kind before raping them.

In the first session, patients frequently wonder, "Can I live through this?" They can be so frightened that they scan the room for escape routes— the door, the window—fearing that you might trap and hurt them. I regularly position my chair so as to not block the door, so that the patients feel able to flee if necessary. Many of them will not consciously remember anything that was said during the first session, yet at the same time it is stored for future use. What they will remember is that they lived through it. Witnessing how easily startled and frightened they are, I find myself afraid of doing anything that might disturb, literally to the point where I try not to move or breathe.

SEXUALIZED BEHAVIOR AND FEELINGS

Many patients I have treated have had as their primary or secondary trauma sexual abuse, or they have sexualized another type of trauma as a way of keeping it at bay. One of the first tests might be to see if the therapist will sexually exploit the patient. It is as if the patient is saying, "If you are going to hurt me, let's get it over with and not waste time; it will be more devastating if you do it later, because I will feel more like a sucker for having hoped you'd be different." For example, female victims often have been taught to provide males with sexual stimulation. Thus they will behave seductively toward the male therapist. I experienced this in Ann's coquettish manner. She wanted me to accept her into treatment and felt sexualized behavior made this more likely.

I focus on sexual feelings in the countertransference; this is an area of great difficulty in working with sexually abused patients. There is a paucity of open discussion of therapists' sexual feelings in the professional literature. This silence does not give therapists support in normalizing these feelings; it also interferes with their ability to fully understand what transpires in the treatment process. This issue is important because therapists' silence and lack of training can lead to repetition and the acting out of unexplored feelings. Because of their vulnerabilities, patients who have been abused in childhood can be further exploited by psychiatrists, psychotherapists, caregivers, and teachers.

Sexual behavior and feelings can have a great number of meanings for both therapists and patients. For example, sex can be employed by the patient, the therapist, or the two together colluding to cover over or distract from the patient's pain; the patient may use sex to maintain self-cohesion, to assert or evidence his or her power, or to seek revenge. Therapists may use sexualized behavior to meet any number of their needs: for power, to feel important, to manage the overwhelming affects (especially the feelings of helplessness generated by listening to such mistreatment), and/or to feel loved. Many sexually abused patients have learned to provide sex to authority figures, especially male ones. Male therapists and their female patients may attempt to cover up many vulnerable feelings with the use of sexualization and anger.

Seductive behavior is common among sexually abused patients and usually occurs early in treatment, manifested by very revealing clothes, sexualized behavior, and coquettishness.

> The first thing that a female patient did when I met her was to look at my groin and lick her lips. Another woman wore a short skirt to the first session; as soon as the session began, she opened her legs wide.

This type of behavior can occur in male patients as well. Here is an especially upsetting experience:

> One young boy, seen for an evaluation, played appropriately with his mother in the therapy room. When I asked his mother to leave the session so that I could spend some time alone with him, he did not protest. When she was out of the room he pulled his pants down and bent over, presenting his behind to me. This is what he had learned to do when alone with a male. I said, "Please pull your pants up." I had a number of reactions to this little boy, including disbelief. The lasting feeling was of sadness about what must have happened to this innocent child.

The therapist's reaction to sexual provocations can be strong. This type of behavior causes some therapists to inappropriately respond sexually to these patients. This is what Ferenczi (1933) calls a "confusion of tongues," where the patients' cry for help and love, along with their hope that the therapist can contain their pain, is misperceived as a sexual advance. When this happens, the patient is then retraumatized and the therapist is bewildered by the patient's intense distress. What has occurred is that the therapist has forgotten his or her role, and has become embroiled in the reenactment of the original trauma. In responding to such overtures in a sexual manner, the therapist's needs have taken precedence over what should be a focus on the patient's welfare.

Sexual intercourse between a patient and the therapist is clearly inappropriate. What should therapists do when they find themselves sexually aroused by a patient? What if the patient is watching the therapist to see if he is aroused when she repeatedly describes sexual experiences? The therapist may wonder if the patient is doing this on purpose, to provide him with sexual stimulation, as Scheherazade did to the sultan to save her life. The patient may perceive the therapist as dangerous. These patients feel that their emotional and even their physical existence may depend on the therapist's approval and on maintaining the tie to the attachment figure.

In addition to these defensive maneuvers to sexually stimulate the therapist, one must consider the seductions of praise (idealization), anger, submission, helplessness, the offerings of gifts, meeting the needs of the therapist, and making referrals to the therapist. How do therapists determine what the appropriate boundaries are? Ann's use of flattery was very effective with me. How can the therapist be conscious of the patient's seductions and defensive appeasement, and distinguish them from the love and strength of increased self-esteem and a healing connection to the therapist? The therapist may be aware of the patient's manipulations but enjoy them too much to explore them. Therapists need to self-monitor and explore themselves regularly. But interpreting or exploring these actions with the patient too early in treatment can provoke anxiety, shame, and humiliation.

Usually when therapists are open, nondefensive, and nonexploitive, patients gradually express their deeper feelings; testing and defensive behaviors tend to dissolve. For example, to deal with the immediate sexualized behavior, therapists can ask the patients what they are feeling and in what part of their body they experience these feelings. This is usually enough to help patients turn their enactment into the expression of a specific affect state. We all have two choices: to sit with our feelings and become aware of them, or to act them out as a way of avoiding them.

CASE ILLUSTRATIONS

Ann's case material* illustrates the opening phase of treatment, and the defensive maneuvers she used to test the first question: "Will you hurt, ignore, or help?"

> In the first session, I was immediately struck by Ann's coquettish manner and felt attracted to her. I saw her in the waiting room, and she saw me, and many thoughts and reactions surged through each of us. I saw her mind racing, body movements communicating so much about hopes, expectations, and our power relationship.
>
> She seemed to be looking everywhere at once. She told me that she was starting to have memories of her father and grandfather molesting her. I listened carefully.
>
> Her previous therapist, whom she had seen for ten months, had insisted that her memories were experiences from a past life, and had explored these "past lives." I indicated surprise. As Ann gained the courage of her convictions about these memories, she felt that she had to leave her previous therapist. She told me that she had been referred to me by another abuse survivor, who said I was wonderful, an expert, and someone who would believe her. I felt flattered. She told me how very nervous she was. My heart went out to her. I agreed to my lowest fee in a long time.
>
> The session was filled with intense fear and hope. It was very exciting to be embarking on a new relationship. It felt akin to an impending marriage. These patients become important to me and remain part of my life for years.

*Sections of Ann's case material in this chapter and in Chapter 10 were previously published in "Unlocking Incest Memories: Preoedipal Transference, Countertransference, and the Body" by S. D. Perlman, in the *Journal of the American Academy of Psychoanalysis* 21(3):363–386, copyright © 1993 by the American Academy of Psychoanalysis and used by permission.

To illustrate the process by which I deal with the intense emotions set off by graphic sexual material, I will reconstruct the process I went through with Ann.

I was aware of Ann telling me about the sexual molestation. I increasingly became aware of her body. I asked myself, Is this a sexual feeling I am having? I wished it would go away. At the same time I felt potent and powerful.

I thought, maybe I am bad for being aroused. This is ridiculous. I feel like a criminal. But I am a therapist! Identification with my professional role anchored me in the midst of my powerful affective experience. This role reinforced my own tendency to use my intellect as a way of surviving emotional storms. I would begin to think about my analysis and this would soothe me, and then I would be able to use my mind again. In my analysis I had come to realize that, as a child, I learned to conquer fear by listening to the upset person's pain and frustrations and decentering from my own fearful experience. In my family, any behavior of mine could set off a violent rampage. I learned to leave my fearful body and center on my mind, to use my intellect to maneuver out of the situation. I had learned the basic stance and task of a therapist, to make contact with the emotional experience of another person, and to gain some distance and perspective on the situation, to analyze it.

The ability to oscillate between these two states enables therapists to use both affective empathic immersion and intellectual perspective to guide their behavior with patients.

Feeling contained once again, I could begin to explore the psychological meanings of the therapeutic situation by using free association, synthesis of associations, and dream interpretation, all of which I had learned in my personal treatment. I used all these techniques to bolster the intellectualizing tendency that I had developed in childhood. At this point in Ann's session, I remembered a childhood experience. An older woman neighbor caught me, at age 6, in sexual play with a little girl neighbor and my sister. She told my parents and, I was sure, everyone else in the neighborhood. For months, each time she saw me she pointed her finger at me as if to say, "Criminal, dirty person." I avoided going outside for a long time. The shame of this experience still lurks inside me. There is freedom in realizing that my feelings of being a criminal because of my sexual impulses derive from my past. I had to let the past go to be present with my patient. This realization helped me regain the therapeutic stance and ask myself, What do these feelings mean about Ann and our relationship?

I told myself that I needed my emotions as useful data in diagnosing Ann's problem. When meeting a new patient, I usually have very specific reactions of anxiety and a desire to please. This anxiety is antithetical to feelings of sexual arousal. So blatant sexual provocation would need to occur for me to have a sexual response in the initial sessions with a patient. Over the years of seeing sexually abused adults and children, I have come to realize that if I become aroused in the first session, it is likely a sign that the patient is a sexual abuse survivor. (Other sexually abused patients may present themselves as asexual to protect themselves.) This was one more piece of data that validated Ann's reports of sexual abuse. It allowed me to empathize with her experience, to try to imagine what she might be doing and feeling. I wondered: Does she feel sexually excited? Her reactions to her sexual feelings were probably complex: a source of power, danger, and guilt. Does she feel that her sexuality is out of her control, that she is a criminal and innately bad? When these sexual feelings are triggered, does she feel unable to think, does she need some way to separate herself from the feelings so she can think again?

Looking back after more experience in treating these patients and in supervising other therapists, I realize that my reactions were not unusual. I have seen some gender differences in the countertransference reactions. Males seem more vulnerable to sexualizing their own countertransferences. Sexual and angry feelings may be more comfortable for many males than nurturance, which is sometimes associated with lack of power. These more vulnerable and softer feelings can be more threatening because they are associated with being feminine or weak. Female therapists may overnurture, at times to the detriment of the exploration of the patient's experience and the development of his or her sense of competency.

As I have had more experience with sexualized behavior within therapy sessions, I have become more aware and more immune. I quickly notice what patients are doing to sexualize a situation. I focus on how patients are feeling with me at each moment. I help patients to express their fears, and this reduces the whole sexual and usually unconscious dynamic. Once patients can tell me that they are both afraid and desperately in need of help, the sexual feelings lessen and are replaced by deeper needs for nurturance.

I saw Ann twice a week for two months as memories began emerging rapidly. She needed more frequent sessions to integrate these power-ful memories. This was the point at which the issues of fee, her need for more frequent sessions, and my need for a supervised case were all negotiated.

I tried to stay aware of how frightened she was in all situations, es-pecially in the budding intimacy of analysis. The deepening process aroused her fear that I would treat her as her father did; in her view, pain and violence were inevitable in intimacy and love. She was con-vinced that she was the bad one, the cause of the other's mistreatment of her; she would, through her emotional needs, turn others into mon-sters like her abusive father, her neglectful mother, or her ridiculing sib-ling.

Constantly experiencing her fear took a toll on me. I felt it was un-fair. I was not her father. I would show her that not all men are bad. Why could she not take that in? Why did I have to suffer for the misdeeds of her father and grandfather? At times I would lose connection with this fearful reality and, with relief, unconsciously choose to relate not to the person she was but to the person she tried to be—someone happy and grateful, who saw me as a wonderful guy. Only with effort could I return to her fear. With this return came a familiar stiffness in my neck. Her anxieties triggered my own past fear of destruction. Her fear also brought to my consciousness the horror of what had been done to her, arousing my sadness and outrage as well as uncertainty: Was I the terrible person she imagined? My fear of being an evil person, which came from my own history of abuse, was confirmed for me in these moments by the Ann's intense reactions. I needed to explore this with my own analyst.

The following dream illustrates the way Ann's material set loose my old traumatic reactions: The world is being invaded by monsters from other worlds. Disease is killing off a lot of people. Ann and I are escaping together in my car. I drop her off at her father's place and keep contact.

This dream illustrates how her material stimulated my fears that the world was a dangerous place, and that her material was invading me. I tried as best I could to save both of us. But in this moment of the dream I felt that to save her was too dangerous to my well-being. I had to abandon her to her father or, metaphorically, to her own fears and traumas. Yet I felt guilty about it and feared for her well-being.

My dream illustrates how difficult it is to stay present and connected when a patient reports traumatic experiences. These reports often activate the therapists' own fears and traumas, forcing them to choose whether to explore their own reactions or to push the patient away. This is a moment-to-moment struggle that needs to be carefully monitored by patients and therapists.

Trauma survivors hope for an experience in which they can be reborn, but this hope and the opening to be reborn are always linked to the possibility of retraumatization. As the patient and therapist become aware of the immensity of the patient's needs, both are at risk of being overwhelmed. This is illustrated in the following vignette, in which Ann represents herself as an unborn starving fetus.

Ann's basic self-image was revealed in an early dream, which she reported four months into analysis. This dream uncovered her core self-image and she was afraid that if I knew how damaged and needy she was, I would abandon her. In the dream, she was a pregnant unborn fetus left to starve. After telling me the dream, she then cried out, "I never had a chance! No one ever took care of me. Why did they all do that to me?"

Her fear that she would overwhelm me was a challenge to my ability to stay with her experience. I felt sad for her, a basically good person who had been tortured as a child. Sometimes, away from session, I would find myself on the verge of crying about what had happened to her. This sadness was a large part of my motivation to help her.

A CLINICAL EXAMPLE OF MANAGEMENT
OF THE FEAR

The patient who has been abused or traumatized frequently expects the therapist to become a perpetrator. It took years for many of these patients to become less frightened of me. Any alteration in the process can raise the fear that the therapist will change and exploit or abandon them. For example, something as simple as a haircut may trigger old fears. If office furniture is changed, this too can set off fear.

I had signed a lease for a new office. I told many of my patients about the move two months in advance. I told them where and when I was moving. Their reaction was explored; if they felt no major anxiety about the move, I would listen for their associations and possibly comment that some discomfort was to be expected. If their associations and anxiety level warranted it, I would make a specific interpretation, possibly about loss experiences that may have been reactivated by the move.

The office move was potentially much more upsetting for trauma survivors. I told them three months in advance, encouraged them to drive by or visit the new location, and if they wished even go into the building and sit in the waiting room. In the weeks before the move, while the new office was empty, I met each of these patients at the new office and gave them a tour. I asked them for advice about what they would want in the new office, which pieces of furniture were important to them, and where to place them. I tried to turn a situation in which they had no control and felt helplessness into one in which they could help plan and participate. Even with these precautions, the fears emerged and took many months to abate. It was as if treatment had to start all over again, as was evidenced by cancellations and the recurrence of old symptoms or traumatic reactions.

In summary, dealing effectively with the trauma survivor's fears and needs for self-protection is a critical first step in treatment. Such patients try early on to understand, assess, and test therapists, using all their automatic self-protective strategies to see if the therapist is going to hurt or betray them. These automatic adaptations have been helpful to them in the past. For many of these persons their most enduring injuries have been caused by the people closest to them; yet the ultimate source of help must also come in intimate relationships. Caught between a rock and a hard place, the patient is frequently paralyzed. Their self-protective acts can trigger corresponding reactions in the therapist—for example, surprise at the patient's fear, not noticing the intensity of the fear, or the arousal of the therapist's own emotions and conflicts. The therapist can become totally caught up in the testing behavior of patients, and miss the centrality of their fear, and their desperate need of help. Patients can then feel misunderstood and retraumatized. Therapists, who wish to be helpers, typically don't want to know when the patient sees them as dangerous, and as a potential abusers, and may instead attend to the patient's praises or gifts. Yet what patients need most is for someone to understand their intense fear of being hurt again, and to recognize their desperate longing for help.

CHAPTER 8

Can I Take Control Over My Own Physical and Emotional Needs?

Most people learn to regulate themselves in childhood in the context of attachment to caregivers (Beebe and Lachmann 1988, Bowlby 1988, Lichtenberg 1983, Stern 1985, Winnicott 1972c). The first lessons in containing and modulating one's feelings and body states are learned as the parent engages the child in helping the child to eat, self-soothe, and sleep. This self-regulating relationship with the therapist leads to similar learning. Eventually such regulation becomes internalized. Once they are securely attached to the therapist, the experience of being regulated and soothed by the therapist is or can be evoked in the patient. This is known in self psychology as the selfobject or selfobject function of the therapist (Kohut 1971, 1977, 1981, 1984). Some patients are fearful of allowing such interdependence with the therapist, while others will feel that their very emotional survival depends on maintaining the connection to the therapist. Slowly, patients can learn to do a large part of this self-regulation on their own.

Trauma survivors spend a great deal of energy maintaining their bodily integrity. Containing and coalescing their emotions, images, and fantasies, along with corresponding bodily sensations, can be an all-consuming task. Many times they are not able to deal with other goals or life tasks. They can be fixated at the level of physical-bodily experience survival, and have great difficulty articulating experience at other levels. One infers this with some patients from the observation that such patients can describe body pain and physical symptoms, but not emotions. Knowing this, the therapist must work to help the patient develop the cognitive means for self-articulation.

FLOODING

Sexually abused and traumatized patients are often unaware and unable to control the affects set loose in them in new and threatening situations, like that of meeting a therapist for the first time. Some of them may have developed self-regulation skills that trauma has subsequently disrupted. Others may have had traumatic experiences at such an early stage of development that these skills never developed. Many of these patients have had the experience of invasion and violation of their bodies and minds, and as a result have little sense of self-ownership and control over themselves. Many have survived by orienting themselves to the needs of people with power over them, who needed these patients to submit to their needs. This then has become a style of functioning for these patients. This constant state of fear and arousal results in a lack of awareness of their own internal states. For example, hunger, fatigue, and other biological needs may not be fully regulated and understood by the patient (van der Kolk and Fisler 1994, van der Kolk et al. 1996). A more complex understanding of their own emotions and arousal levels often does not exist. They are frequently in a state of hyperalertness, ready to flee, fight, or freeze during most of their waking hours and, to some degree, while sleeping. This leaves no tolerance for increased arousal because they are already on the verge of flooding and overstimulation. When patients are flooded they cannot process verbal communications. The higher brain functions become impaired. Taking control of one's physical and emotional needs is a major goal of treatment; this ability allows the processing and integration of new information.

SELF-REGULATION: AN IMPORTANT FOCUS FROM THE START OF TREATMENT

I have learned after many years that it is important to deal with the issue of self-regulation from the first session. To do so gives patients a sense that the therapist cares about them in a way that they have rarely felt. Others in their life have probably not realized, or have denied, how profoundly compromised trauma survivors' functioning is on a moment-to-moment basis. Most people take for granted others' ability to regulate arousal levels, to think, and to communicate, but these are impaired with an emotionally flooded person.

I begin to help patients take control over their internal experience by allowing them to have as much control as possible over the therapeutic situation. I explore whether they can hear and understand what I am saying, and whether they are present in the room and can experience their own feelings at the moment. I encourage them to talk or not as they desire. I encourage them to feel free to not answer any question I may ask that they are not prepared to deal with. I encourage them to make decisions about where they would like to sit or even stand. I hand over control of where I sit or stand, whether they can see me, or whether I can see them, if it seems that they need to have this to feel more comfortable. A composite illustration follows:

> An adolescent survivor of brutal incest by his father, as witnessed by others, was referred for treatment. He would not speak to me, yet came on his own for treatment and was always on time. I would comment on how he seemed that day. We sat many times in silence; I would say to him that I respected his right not to speak if he chose, because in so many situations he had felt that he had no choice. I felt frustrated and useless at times. He was truant from school, so I felt that he would not come to session if he did not want to. After months, he finally spoke and said that he chose not to come back any more. I told him that I wanted to talk about what happened to him, but that if he chose not to come back I would respect that. I told him that he could come back at another point in time if he chose. He left therapy. Later one of his friends called to come into treatment. He had been referred by this survivor, who had said to her, "This man can help you."

As therapists, we get a sense of validation when patients produce detailed clinical material. What was important to this patient, however, was what had been missing in his life: respect for his needs as opposed to the needs of another, including the therapist.

When I am making choices in treatment, I often remind myself, "Process over content." I remind myself that my relationship and the way I am behaving toward the patient are more important than the accounts, memories, or insights. The central method of healing is to allow the patient to reexperience the pain and the trauma within the context of a safe relationship. Discovery and insight will come if the patient feels safe and respected. But too much reexperiencing can exhaust and retraumatize the patient.

RELIVING THE TRAUMA IN TREATMENT

Opening up traumatic material can overstimulate patients. A critical part of treatment for these patients is to learn how to soothe themselves, and to manage these states so as to prevent the treatment itself from becoming a traumatic experience. The therapist must watch that the intense pain and horror that the memories arouse are not used by the patient in a self-abusive way. Some patients dive into the material in the hope of getting better quickly. The pacing or titrating of emotional material is essential.

Currently, I would handle the issue of self-regulation in my treatment of Ann differently than I did when I started treating her ten years ago. At that time, I did not understand the importance of self-regulation. I did not closely track Ann's tendency to become flooded; I did not always intervene when an intense state lasted too long. Especially given the amount of traumatic material that she was reliving, I probably should have attempted to slow down the process. I could have done this by helping her to self-soothe and pace herself and by teaching her how to use her dissociation as a technique for self-care. I might have seen her less frequently but in more double sessions. Instead, I pushed for more uncovering, which led to flooding and interfered with her ability to function in the outside world. By pushing to uncover at moments when she was already flooded, I contributed to these periods of reduced functioning.

By letting patients have more control in sessions, therapists give up some of their own. At a presentation I talked about how I allow some patients to tell me where to sit. A well-known therapist stated he could never let a patient make those decisions for him, because it would make him too uncomfortable. We all need to determine our limits and limitations. But it is my hope that we can explore situations that make us uncomfortable and understand them, as we also explore the roots and meanings of the patient's needs. Then we are in a better position to decide how to respond. From my roots in humanistic psychology, I still believe in patients' innate desire to get better, and that in many situations they know what they need better than I do.

CONTINUOUS SENSE OF CONNECTION, AND SESSION ENDINGS

Session endings are frequently difficult for trauma patients, and can help or hinder their connection with the therapist. Issues of abandonment and caring are prominent. For example, they may become so caught up in reliving a past trauma that the end of a session comes as a jolt. It is extremely important to help them leave the office in a contained state and reoriented to the outside world they are about to rejoin. It sometimes happens that these patients leave session in a "young state of being" and, preoccupied with childhood memories, have gotten into car accidents. Reorienting the patient to current reality lessens these types of risks.

The ending of session may need to be discussed five, ten, or fifteen minutes before the time is up. Sometimes it is important to let patients know how much time remains in the session. The therapist can begin telling patients that it is time to begin putting the difficult material away for now and orienting themselves to the outside world. If patients have trouble reorienting to the present, and to the tasks of everyday functioning, the therapist can ask about how much of the material is put away, and then a few minutes later ask again. This creates some perspective on the process of containing traumatic material. This approach helps patients develop a systematic way to contain flooding. Patients need time to get into traumatic material and time to work their way out; some may need double sessions.

> A male patient, held down and sodomized by at least one male in his family, experienced a good deal of his therapy as "sodomization." He reexperienced the trauma as if it were happening in the moment, with the therapist as perpetrator. Many times I felt bad and guilty in my dealings with this man; I felt the impulse to protest, "I did not do anything, I'm trying to help you!" To reduce his anxiety to manageable proportions, and also reduce my own disturbing reactions, I allowed him as much control as possible. He called and set up each appointment separately, with no clear commitment as to when he would return. He told me where to sit and whether I could look at him. He walked around the office at times and used other forms of physical activity to reduce his anxiety, proving to himself he was not being held down. He tended to end sessions slightly early as a way of taking control. We talked often about strategies for settling himself down in social situations, where he often panicked because he felt trapped. Treatment needed to proceed slowly, or he would feel enslaved, meaning sodomized, by me. At the same time, he expressed deep affection and a sense of connection to me. He often left messages on my answering machine about his emotional state, an experience that helped calm him.

THE MEANING OF SELF-ASSERTION

Many abused and traumatized patients have difficulty setting limits on others or taking care of themselves because such assertive actions arouse fears that they will be abused. To assert their needs is to say no to the abusive other and, thus, to risk retaliation. At these moments patients may panic and need more connection to the therapist.

> Each time Ann took a step toward growth and/or assertion, she needed to check back with me. When she wrote a letter terminating a relationship with an abusive friend of long standing, she called me in a panic,

saying she had a great deal of bodily pain. I told her that even though she was letting go of this person, I was still strongly connected to her. When I asked her what came to mind about the body pain, she said that she felt all alone; she then remembered being in the hospital after her father violently abused her, when her jaw had to be wired shut and her eyes covered, and other people did not know for days whether she was conscious. On the phone she asked, "Could you give me a pill to fix it all?" I said, "I am sending it to you over the phone; I'd like you to swallow it now." I heard a gulp, and she laughed. She said in a playful happy voice, "I feel like I can do cartwheels now."

In summary, being aware of and taking control over one's physical and emotional needs, sometimes called self-regulation, is a crucial but not fully appreciated aspect of treatment. This lesson is especially important for severely traumatized and abused patients, who can be flooded with affect, and rarely see themselves as agents of initiative and control. Without attention to the patients' emotional and physical regulation, the therapist can unwittingly contribute to their being overwhelmed by the process.

THERAPIST SELF-CARE

Lack of awareness and control over one's physical and emotional needs can be a problem for both patients and therapists, especially therapists new to working with trauma survivors. (Some related issues were discussed in Chapter 5 and more will be discussed in Part III.) Therapists must set limits when they are overwhelmed by the patients' material. This is necessary to prevent retaliatory acting out that can endanger the relationship. Therapists need consultations and vacations.

One purpose of this book is to make therapists more aware of the demands of the treatment process. There needs to be some balance between the needs of the patient and of the therapist. We can be more effective if we know what this work can touch off in us. The demands of these patients force us to learn limit-setting, lest we become depleted. I have learned this lesson the hard way, and I have finally learned to say, "I understand and hear that you need that from me, but right now I am unable to provide it." This has been necessary in dealing with late-night calls, physical holding, fee reductions, weekend sessions, and related issues. Rather than blame the patients for their needs, I may explain that I must say no to this particular demand but will continue to help them over the long haul. Without commenting on it at the time to the patient, it is very important to model self-regulation and limit-setting. In extreme situations, I have used an additional therapist to see the patient while I was on vacations or during times of crisis when I or the patient felt in need of additional help. This can be experienced by the therapist as a narcissistic injury—"Why am I not good enough?"—and by patients as proof of their badness. These feelings need to be explored and interpreted.

CHAPTER 9

Can You Hear Me?

Resolutions of patients' central questions build on one another. If the therapist can help the patients communicate about their own fear and need for soothing and caregiving, they will begin to feel heard.

This last question in the first stage of treatment can be thought of as, "Can I confront you with what I really feel, and will you accept it as having value?" Many times this confrontation targets the therapists' uncomfortable feelings. Many patients need to see that therapists will look within and accept the patients' feelings and thoughts.

It is common for trauma survivors to discover that others do not want to hear what happened to them. For example, it may be too painful for the listener (Herman 1992). In sexual abuse it is typically even more complicated. These patients have usually been ignored, told they were not worth listening to, or told that they were crazy or liars when they attempted to reveal their abuse experiences (Hanks et al. 1988, *Los Angeles Times* study 1985). Many of them assume that their ideas and feelings will never be heard or validated. Their very sense of existence is undermined.

Being heard is a rare experience for many of these people, who have been so profoundly invalidated. Kohut, the founder of self psychology, reasserted in his last taped interview (Kohut 1981) that the empathic experience of being heard has healing effects in itself.

In treatment, patients are usually assessing whether therapists can hear their pain and needs, and allow them to speak, asking "Can you hear me?" Here the patients are asking, Can therapists understand and let exist what is said? Can therapists acknowledge their own part in the interaction? Trauma survivors typically become hypervigilant, especially about the emotional states of others; they interpret such states as warning signs of disaster. Many of these patients sense what therapists are thinking and feeling even before the therapists do. This can be disconcerting, and therapists may feel invaded, unable to hide. Therapists confronted with their own feelings may wish to deny them to protect their privacy. If the therapists remain reserved, patients may mistrust their own sense of reality. When there is silence or ambiguity, these patients usually assume that the therapists are thinking something negative. Unless corrected, they believe the worst, increasing their level of fear.

As a guideline, one should not deny patients' observations, especially if they are accurate. Exploring the patients' feelings without having to confirm or deny them can give both parties a chance to understand their experience more fully. This can be done by asking, "Was there anything I did or said that made you think that?" and then, "What is it like to think that I feel that way?" At times, however, therapists may need to acknowledge the accuracy of patient's perceptions and deal with the consequences.

The following vignette illustrates the impact of the patients' perceptiveness on the therapeutic experience. It also shows how a specific sexual enactment was difficult for me to process earlier in my work, due to my own guilt and shame. Once I became more fully aware of my own reactions, such situations were much easier to manage. These patients were then able to sense that I could see through the defensive sexualization to the injured little child inside.

> Ann was often aware of my thoughts and anger even before I was. She would confront me, saying, "You are thinking and feeling something; I can tell." She usually had a clear idea of what I was thinking, which my

questions confirmed. I initially wanted to hide from her. There were many issues I wished not to deal with, such as my anger over unpaid fees, or my looking at her legs. I would try to avoid acknowledging these feelings. This would result in her emotionally collapsing before my eyes. She would feel like her reality did not exist unless I confirmed it. Exploring this feeling with her did not seem to be enough. Her confidence in her own perceptions seemed at stake. She would also become fearful that she could not trust other aspects of our relationship. When I realized how badly she took my passive nonconfirmations of her perceptions, I felt trapped. I felt forced to tell her what I was experiencing. This was very difficult for me because I was ashamed of some of my reactions to her, particularly sexual feelings. Once I was willing to acknowledge my feelings and explore her reactions, however, she became revitalized; at times she was afraid and angry but felt alive, open, and expressive. This led to an exploration of her conflictual feelings about her sexuality and her body; about wanting my attention and, at the same time, fearing it. It led to discussions of many past situations where she felt she had no value if she was not a desired sexual object, as evidenced by her revealing dress and her history of not being able to say no to a man's sexual advances. It was also validating for her to learn that she could be attractive and have the power to decide how involved she became with a man.

Over time, I became less critical of my reactions, and more comfortable with my sexuality even when it dominated my awareness. Only after overcoming my shame did I start to be aware that Ann was being sexually provocative with me. For example, when she was afraid of my rage, she would behave seductively as a defensive maneuver. We explored those moments and motives.

Interpreting sexual feelings too early can make patients feel criticized, leading to intense feelings of shame. In time I began to offer interpretations such as, "Sometimes when you are scared you automatically try to give me what you think I want, so you will be safe." "Many times you don't feel old enough to have sexual feelings." "These sexual feelings sometimes feel good and other times feel too scary." "You feel you must provide these for me or else I won't continue to help you." "Sometimes you feel worthless except as a sexual object." These interpretations helped Ann to speak more about underlying reactions. Later, it was important to affirm the sense of worth she got from her sexuality, to help her appreciate it, especially when she had an open and loving sexual relationship with a man she was dating.

TWO VIGNETTES

I will present two vignettes. The first, early in my career, illustrates how a difficult countertransference provoked by the patient interfered with my ability to hear this patient and the resulting escalation of the negative interaction. The second illustrates how I was able to listen as a result of managing my own issues, which resulted in a different outcome.

> A 9-year-old boy was brought in for behavioral problems at school. It emerged that he had been sexually abused. He would drool on me, grab my penis, and otherwise intrude on my body.
>
> At the time I did not fully understand these intrusions as enactments of his abuse. They made me feel uncomfortable and weird. I asked myself, Was there a part of me that was stimulated? Mostly I felt vulnerable and attacked.
>
> He would tear at my new couch, and made a hole in it. This and other intrusions made me angry, but I did not know what to do with this feeling. Sometimes I interpreted his anger when he actually was sad, and it was my anger. In response, he would become sexually excited. He had associated male authority figures' anger with sexuality. At times my anger would come out as harshness and lack of empathy.
>
> In one session, the boy talked about being made fun of at school. I focused away from his humiliation and toward how he had to follow the rules in class. He began tearing at my couch again, widening the hole. Again I missed his pain, saying, "You are angry at me." He gave a sexually excited laugh, associating a male's anger with sexuality. After I told him not to tear the couch, he playfully tried to wrestle with me. I became nervous: this was usually when he would try to grab my penis and drool on me. I said, "I am not willing to wrestle, and you are trying to get my

attention by having sexual contact." This was closer to his pain, but it did not stop his sexual advance; as I remained in my seat, he lay on the ground and pulled his pants down, trying to pull my hand to his buttocks. At the same time he was yelling, "Get off of me! Get off of me!" He began to show me aspects of the original trauma, because my interpretation had come closer to his pain. I told him to pull his pants up.

Each time I misconstrued his sadness and humiliation he escalated the aggression while enacting parts of his trauma. This pattern can be present with adult patients who have been sexually abused. They try to disguise and distract others from their underlying feelings with words, but children will act out the trauma more directly. Upon self-analysis I remembered how other children used to ridicule and humiliate me at school, and realized that this experience may have interfered with my ability to focus on this patient's pain. If I had made an interpretation such as, "I think you are trying to show me what happened to you and how it felt," I believe he would have felt more understood and contained.

The following dream illustrates the self-analysis I did to help this boy: I am trying to help this 9-year-old boy who feels lonely, fat, and rejected. He turns on me and threatens suicide to hurt me when I say I am leaving. I start to cry, saying, "I tried to help him because I feel so lonely and bad, too."

I had to face the pain and the feelings from my own childhood that this boy's pain brought up in me, and stay with him as he experienced his sadness and anger. I had to contain my feelings toward his rage.

This second case illustrates how trauma and abuse ripples through a person's social network, and from one generation to the next. It illustrates how the opening up of one person to healing can also have a rippling effect.

The family had been referred because the boy, of kindergarten age, wanted to be a girl. He was entwined with his mother, who had been physically and sexually abused by her father. She hated and feared men. I wondered whether this child, to be safe with his mother, felt that he had to be a girl because he saw what happened to his older brother. This older brother, who was hypermasculine and bonded with the father, was physically mistreated by mother. The father avoided conflict and emotions, and taught the children denial by saying, "You don't re-ally mean that." In addition to my work with the child and family, the mother had an individual therapist.

In contrast to the example of the boy who would grab me, I was able to be more open to this family's pain. Concurrently, in my own analysis, I was working on my childhood abuse. Even with this support, I noticed that I gave a nervous laugh whenever the violence in this family reminded me of my own experience.

To sit with this mother was to sit with terror. Some time later, I asked her about her experience of the first session. She said that during the session she could not hear or remember anything I said, but that she survived it. At the same time, she observed that she could never under-stand why people were afraid of being beaten or found it painful. When I asked how she had become that way, she said, "Beats me." Because I could listen, she was able to focus on the phrase "Beats me" and talk of her father beating her.

As this woman became more aware of how her father had beaten and sexually abused her, her fear of hurting her son became a major concern. She and her son kept themselves physically separate in ses-sions. But, as therapy progressed, her empathy for her son grew. We consulted the child abuse hotline, which advised us that she had not yet crossed the line to actual abuse.

In one session, the mother was withdrawn, and covered herself with a pillow. Her older son was busy drawing a monster that was cutting off people's heads with a chainsaw. Asked about the picture, he said the monster enjoyed killing. I related it to his mom and dad, and he said he wanted the monster to kill his mom. At this moment he became afraid of his mother. We explored this fear, and the mother reassured him that it was all right to feel that way.

I could see how upset his mother was. She could not find words to express her feelings, so I tried to express them for her and let her tell me if I was accurate. We talked of her pain for having hurt him, of her pain for having been hurt by her father, and of her sadness that her son had experienced some of the same pain at her hands. The mother re-moved her shoe and sock, and kept rubbing her son's leg with her foot. He then took off his shoes and socks, and they rubbed feet.

On ten-year follow-up, the mother has continued in treatment with another therapist. In general, she had improved, but was still struggling with the same issues. Her sons were doing very well. I felt sad that the mother was still struggling, but heartened about the improvement in the next generation.

By working on my own issues, I could more effectively help this family. Genuine intimacy grew within each dyad in the family and with me. Experiences like this one gave me hope.

In summary, therapists must learn to contain their own emotions in order to accompany patients back to their trauma experiences. When this is done, it is possible to integrate the experience of trauma within the shared space and the patient.

Second Stage of Treatment: Deep Experience

During the first stage of successful treatment patients have begun to feel some safety and connection with the therapist. It is hoped that patients feel heard, and have learned to contain or regulate their emotions and body experiences enough to think and experience themselves. This forms the groundwork for patients to explore deeper aspects of their experience.

Patients may already be aware of these aspects, or may only be able to face them with the support of the therapist. In both cases patients usually are not fully aware of the influence these issues are having in their lives.

In the second stage of treatment, where the patient is in a deeper process, the previous questions continue to be important, with additional questions now moving periodically to the foreground. Not all patients will deal with all questions directly in treatment, and isolated questions may not be relevant to a specific patient. Detailed clinical and personal material is used to illustrate each stage and question.

Each of these questions, as those of Stage 1, represents an opening to an area of deeper experience. The following openings are not

clearly a requirement for the mobilization of the deep maternal transference. This powerful transference can exist even with problems in
treatment and levels of denial and disconfirmation. This is a tribute
to the adaptiveness of these patients to survive difficult situations.
Yet without these next levels of listening and validation, many patients leave or can be hurt by treatment.

"Can you listen to the trauma and validate me?" Here patients long
to have someone listen to what they believe has happened and
not deny their experience. Too often others have denied their experience, especially around their trauma and its graphic details.
This usually has stopped patients from integrating their experience into the narrative of their own life. With the therapist's
mirroring, patients are able to experience themselves as the valid
owner of thoughts and feelings as well.

"Am I lovable?"—Feeling deep love and bonding. Opening to these
experiences exposes the basic feelings of being bad and unloved
and apart from other people, which is a core experience for most
traumatized patients. Even though the lost childhood can never
be reclaimed, the patient needs some feelings of being loved, valued, and connected to the therapist in a way that allows the patient to psychically integrate. Central to the patient at some critical
moments of the treatment is the patient's need to feel emotionally connected to the therapist in a very deep and continuous way.
This is in part the result of a need to feel a oneness with the therapist and/or being emotionally dependent on the therapist for one's
psychic regulation.

"Can you see me?"—Discontinuous and shattered existence. This opening encompasses the discontinuous experience of the patient. This
aspect of human functioning is regaining acceptance. Most splits
contain unbearable affective experiences. Ferenczi (1933) wrote,
"there is neither shock nor fright without some splitting of the
personality" (p 164). Thus, trauma survivors by definition are
probably split up or shattered in their experience of themselves
in some respect. This does not allow cohesive functioning. To
heal, the splits must be explored and brought together.

"*Who is bad and who is the abuser?*" This opening continues to explore the patient's feeling of badness and explores how the splits and unbearable experiences are acted out in the patient's life and in treatment. It also highlights the difficulties the therapist experiences in tolerating the patient's different, and often provocative, transferences and enactments.

"*Is this my body?*"—*Touch*. We live in and experience life through our body. Trauma usually results in the patient's being overwhelmed and not able to process the experience. Then the experience is stored in pieces in sensations and body experiences. Patients need help reclaiming their bodies and the deep sensual experiences of the past (body memories) and present.

"*Can you believe in ritual abuse?*" This is an area of heated debate. The therapist may be faced with patients who believe they are victims of this type of abuse. The emotional reactions of the therapist need to be understood and explored as well as the patient's experience of these reactions. The therapist can take several possible stances in relation to the patient's material, each of which is explored below.

CHAPTER 10

Can You Listen to the Trauma and Validate Me?

"Can you listen to the trauma and validate me?" is a complicated question that has two parts. The first part is "Can you hear about the trauma and its horrors?" Here patients are asking whether therapists can tolerate, comprehend, and resonate with the intensity of the trauma and the responses others had to the patient after the trauma. Some therapists who can listen and hear about many other issues have special difficulties with the details of trauma and abuse. The second part is "Can you believe me?" This a crucial question, because the trauma has become an organizing experience around which many aspects of the patient's personality have developed (Hamilton 1989). The trauma cannot be reworked effectively until it has been acknowledged and reexperienced in a supportive environment. The issue of being believed is intrinsic to the patients' ability to experience themselves as valid centers of thought that can be maintained in the face of others' thoughts. This is frequently manifested in chronic self-doubting.

CAN YOU HEAR ABOUT THE TRAUMA AND ITS HORRORS?

Patients typically have faced unreceptive ears when they attempt to speak of their experience. This reinforces the expectation that others do not want to know about such events. My own life experiences affected my readiness to hear; I experienced personal traumas that other people ignored. For example, the school bus accident I described earlier illustrates the cloak of silence maintained by participants and the community. This made me acutely aware of my patients' pain. My experiences also confirmed Herman's (1992) point that after a major trauma even a person with good pretrauma development will disconnect from others in his or her life. At times it is as if part of the survivor has died in the trauma.

Therapists have a choice: to experience the emotions the patient shares, or refuse to share (for example, by interrupting) in those feelings. If the therapist can allow a sustained affective connection to the traumatic material, the patient senses this and will continue the exploration. There is a mutual sensing of tolerances that can facilitate the process. Listening to stories of trauma can frighten therapists. These feelings can be an empathic experiencing of the patient's material, or arise from unresolved issues of their own.

Trauma memories often return in confusing ways. This can be difficult for therapists, who must contain their own need for structure, certainty, and closure. For many trauma survivors, memories first emerge as bodily sensations such as feeling pain, smelling odors, or having bleary eyes. Many times, these physical sensations are followed by a welling up of emotions, fear, and bewilderment. After a time, visual and auditory memories emerge. Next, these patients may experience shock and disbelief, saying, "I must be crazy; this can't be true; my parents were not like this; how could this be?" Patients may prefer to believe that they are crazy, or making these images up, rather than face the implications. At these moments, survivors usually turn to therapists and demand that their therapist confirm their reality. There are often "flashbacks," perceptual experiences of being "back there" in the trauma. Feelings of disgust, shame, and guilt alternate with disbelief; patients may say, "I must be bad, I must have caused it. I must be crazy." If at any time in this process therapists interfere or are unsupportive, the memories may revert back to bodily sensations. If, on the other hand, the therapist remains empathetic, then the work can again proceed toward integration. Eventually, patients tend to mourn the loss of the childhood fantasies they have developed to manage the trauma.

Burland and Raskin (1990) describe the memory retrieval process:

> [Sexual abuse survivors in analysis] who had a long history of more than adequate reality testing and function in life, had gone through a period when they seemed almost borderline in their functioning as their grasp on reality collapsed and their self-doubting and confusion intensified; some even experienced what seemed to be transference psychoses. Once their memories were recovered and acknowledged, the patients' mental status rapidly reverted to its previous, more adequate condition. [p. 38]

Burland and Raskin emphasize patients' need to know that the analyst believes them, that he or she will not retraumatize them by challenging the reality of their reports.

Ann's case illustrates the difficulty of memory reintegration for both patients and therapists.

One memory dominated the opening months of Ann's treatment: difficulty swallowing. She had trouble swallowing for days when she brought into treatment a half-drawn picture (Figure 10–1) of a man entering a child's room at night. She began telling me about the picture.

Notice the man's arm and shadow by the door. At first, she had not known what this image meant. I had chills when I saw the man's shadow.

She then reported pains in her vagina and began groaning. Seeing flashes and hearing noises, she began to cry. She turned to me and asked, "Could this be true?" At these moments, I was asking myself the same question. I wondered, What should I think or say? Sometimes I said, "What do your insides tell you?" but mostly I would say, "Let's explore your experience and over time it will become clear." It was difficult to allow the ambiguity to continue. Over the weeks her confidence in the truth of the memories grew. Over time I told her, "The pieces of the memories seem consistent and fit together." "I have worked with other people to whom this has happened as well." "I believe you." "It's horrible what he did to you." She counted the minutes between sessions. She was afraid that her father, who was still alive, would come to her apartment and kill her. She stopped answering the phone and left her apartment only for therapy sessions and groceries.

Figure 10-1

What eventually emerged was that when she was 3 or 4 years old, her father came home from the war in Vietnam. He burst into her room in the middle of the night, saying, "I'll get you Nammies." He had a gun in his hand. He grabbed her neck and put his penis in her mouth, thrusting and choking her. He ejaculated in her mouth, then shoved his gun into her vagina and said that he was going to kill her. Hurting, she waited to die from the bullet. Then her father started to vomit and ran to the bathroom, staying there while her mother called for him to come out. He kept vomiting and screaming. Her mother put Ann back in bed, wiped the blood off the floor and walked away. Ann does not remember anyone mentioning the experience ever again.

I was horrified and had trouble listening. It made me want to cradle this poor child. I was outraged at her father, and at her mother for not protecting her. Listening to this account brought up painful memories of my own childhood. At rare moments, I interrupted her with detailed questions to delay the flood of feeling. Over time, as I explored my own memories, I interrupted her less frequently.

Ann's material restimulated issues from my own early treatment, particularly rage toward my father. I wondered, How could I be a male if males were like my father, like Ann's father? I did not want to hurt others. My first therapist was a gentle man. My work with him seemed to open up new possibilities. My analyst, this new man, was able to listen. It was scary to say out loud what I really felt about my father. I feared my father's retaliation. When I was a child, my father worked eighty to ninety hours a week to keep us fed. He was a professional boxer, a plumber, a well-connected politician, and a delicatessen owner. He fought in World War II. He was a dynamic and scary figure to me.

With the help of my therapy, I began to remember more and more of the details of my father's abusive conduct. I felt years of anger over the violence. Yet I loved him and was guilt ridden over my continued separation from my family.

This material illustrates that abusive families can have intense and complicated bonding. As a child, I felt allied with my mother against my father. In therapy I began to overcome my inability to think separately from her. I came to view my mother as more destructive and my father as more human than before.

While treating Ann I had nightmares about her abuse and mine. Sometimes I wished she would stop the fear-ridden late-night calls. I became fearful that my wife would be angry at me about the calls. But, to my surprise, my wife did not express too much anger. She greatly appreciated the valuable work I was doing for these patients. Ann felt competitive with my wife for my attention, and hoped at times that I would leave my wife for her. I found this flattering. She also felt relieved, however, that I was "happily married" and therefore less likely to rape her. She developed a transferential experience of my wife as a secondary caregiver.

Listening to the details of abuse can stimulate many reactions in the therapist. Disbelief is common. Therapists may be in a state of shock, having trouble believing that people could do such things to innocent children. Stories of abuse can tap directly into therapists' feelings and fears that people are dangerous. Listening to details of abuse can raise fears for their own children, spouse, or loved ones.

> Ann's treatment stimulated a sense of invasion and terror in me, as well as dredging up my feelings about my father. My dream illustrates this: A Chinese woman, 25 to 30 years old, runs into my home and steals something. She is too fast and gets away. The next time she steals my father's mugs, and I run faster and chase her outside. There is a crazed man waiting in a truck who sees me chasing her, and he comes after me with a hacksaw.

Therapists may be shocked at their reactions to the content, which conflicts with their sense of themselves as caring persons. Hearing stories about how the abuser tied up and raped the helpless child, and exploited her in every possible manner, can stimulate a great deal of conflict and fantasy in therapists.

If therapists cannot contain these upsetting affects, the therapist will interrupt the process. Therapists may stop patients from exploring these memories, try to save the patient from the pain of exploration, or label them as fantasies. Hearing these stories may also stimulate rescue fantasies, the enactment of which may reduce the therapist's anxiety but infantilizes the patient, interfering with the overall treatment process and derailing the uncovering of the memories.

Yet many patients need their memories in order to heal and become whole. After one abused patient recalled difficult memories, she told me that it was important to do so because she felt "more like myself, more solid, more confident although more afraid of the world." This was her life and her past. Acknowledging it made her feel more connected to herself.

Listening to my patients' lives made the world darker for me. I became more cognizant of the damage people can do to each other, and more protective against others' behavior toward me and my loved ones. I became more aware of how hard it is to repair the damage that these people sustain, and of human frailty under massive assault. At the same time, it helped me understand my own life by seeing my experience mirrored back to me in my patients.

DO YOU BELIEVE ME?: CHRONIC SELF-DOUBTING AND REALITY

Therapists have assumptions about what exists, and this directs their readiness to validate and observe. There is a controversy about how much therapist validation a patient needs to work through these issues. Some say the therapist must believe all that is said for some patients to feel validated, and that this concrete demonstration of validity is demanded and required for some patients. It is possible with some patients for the therapist to validate the patients' statements, without fully believing all of them, but this is a very delicate balance. At minimum, to treat sexually abused patients, therapists need to explore the patients' experience of such abuse and be willing to observe its effects.

My stance is that therapists ordinarily do and should believe what patients tell them unless there is some compelling reason not to. This is particularly necessary when treating survivors of sexual abuse and trauma. These patients struggle with their relationship to the images and thoughts that come to them, experiences that have often been invalidated by important people in their life.

Here is an example from Ann's treatment illustrating some of her attempts to receive validation from her family.

Ann's memories of abuse would alternate with mourning for the family she wished she had. Her memories threatened her belief that her family loved and cared for her. As therapy progressed she confronted each member of her family with her memories. At first her father apologized, but when Ann told his new wife, he denied it and verbally attacked her. Her mother also denied Ann's reality and verbally attacked her. Her siblings remembered details of the abuse but refused to discuss it, saying, "Why cause trouble now?" These interactions added to her trauma; she was left with her thoughts and the feeling that she was bad and crazy.

Ann was angry at her mother. She remembered telling her about the abuse several times when she was a child, but her mother ignored her. When Ann was 5 or 6, she remembers her mother taunted her for liking "sex" and "boys." Subsequently, her mother's sister confessed to having been sexually molested by her own father (Ann's mother's father) in the same way as Ann: he would ask her to go for a walk or into the garage, or ask her to play a game; he would touch her, put his penis in her mouth, ejaculate, then take her for ice cream, or give her a nickel, asking her to promise not to tell anyone. Ann believed that her grandfather also sexually molested her mother. Ann's mother always hated men, and said that all a man ever wants is sex. Ann and I both believed that her mother needed to deny Ann's traumatic experiences with incest as a way of denying her own traumatic incest. Although her mother denied it, Ann also remembered witnessing her father beating her mother. Her family's style of neglect, coupled with overenmeshment, resembled that of other abusive families.

Abused and traumatized patients are usually highly attuned to many aspects of therapists' behavior, including their phrasing and tone of voice, and the topics they address and the topics they avoid. Some of these patients sense what therapists are feeling before the therapists are aware of it. When therapists deny having an opinion that patients sense is present, or refuse to express it, patients can experience this as deliberate withholding. Patients are then in a dilemma as to whether they must give up part of their sense of reality, or part of their trust of the therapist's words. Either can be devastating.

Therapists' own experiences often determine their readiness to believe the patient. They must stay aware of personal influences and not impose their own reality on the patient. I have had to monitor and be sensitized to my own traumas and how they have influenced the treatment.

Knowing what it felt like to have my own traumatic experiences ignored made it crucial for me to attend to Ann's thoughts, feelings, and memories. I would not reject her memories of abuse, as others had. I wanted to be the therapist who could help Ann where others had failed.

I had many experiences with my own family that affected my willingness to believe Ann's ideas. The following is one.

My mother had a history of anger and violence toward her children but refused to discuss it. At the time I began to work with Ann, I went to my older brother's wedding. He ignored our mother's demands to do things her way in spending his time and attention, and I told her to leave him alone. Later that day I was videotaping the wedding for my brother. My mother came up to me and began yelling curses at me and threatening to hit me with her raised fist. I videotaped this. The next day I recalled the experience to her and she responded, "I would never say or do anything like that!" I played the tape for my mother. She watched it, then walked away, saying nothing. Later, when I confronted her again, she refused to discuss it. This was a startling example of the power of denial.

Many therapists attempt to verify the occurrence of the abuse reported by their patients. They may be pulled out of their role as a therapist into that of an investigator, seeking certainty about things that they did not witness. These sometimes obsessive attempts to confirm the patients' reality may mirror the patients' struggle.

Many patients reenact their traumas in therapy, with the therapist in the role of perpetrator. The original abusers usually ignored the children's feelings, punishing them and threatening them for telling what happened; they often tell the children that they deserve, want, or enjoy it. In many cases, victims would be threatened by the perpetrator if they told what happened.

Children take in these comments concretely, resulting in odd behaviors and distorted self-images. Many patients are able to draw pictures of the abuse and reenact it, before they are able to talk about it, because drawing and reenacting were not specifically subject to threat of harm. The child's ability to think, speak, and see may be affected in a more general sense as well. Many children (and later as adults) see themselves as deserving of, and causing, bad things to happen, or as a person who must have sex.

In those cases where children did tell others about the abuse, they were usually branded as liars, and given no effective help (Hanks et al. 1988, *Los Angeles Times* study 1985). Therefore, when patients tell therapists about the abuse, they typically expect a negative or punitive response.

Some of the fears of telling may be real. The therapist may be legally bound to file a child abuse report. The original abusers may still be alive, and may carry out their threats when they learn that the victims have reported the abuse to others.

CHRONIC SELF-DOUBTING

One of the most damaging residual effects of sexual abuse is the patient's inability to maintain thoughts in the face of other people's judgments and responses. To focus solely on the chronic self-doubting of the reality of the abuse is to miss this deeper issue, of which the chronic doubting of the abuse is only one manifestation. The patient's inability to hold on to his or her thoughts occurs in many situations in his or her daily life and this interferes with the patient's ability to live proactively.

Abuse survivors need to feel that they own their own reality. Because of their histories, they expect that someone will force another version of reality upon them. Their vacillation as to the reality of their trauma represents a larger struggle to know what is real. Will they be able to express their own perceptions and beliefs? They sometimes fear the expression of their perceptions as counter to the therapist's needs. It is important that they are able to change their minds without the therapists becoming angry or forcing them to be consistent.

Patients may demand that therapists validate the reality of their reports and this may make them feel put on the spot, uncertain about how best to respond. Yet validating reality for these patients is a central part of the healing process. But it is a complicated process.

Ann's chronic self-doubting was illustrated by the memory of her father's gun in her vagina. Her chronic self-doubting did not go away. The following is a transcript of Ann's treatment some years later.

> *Ann*: It's so hard for me to believe all that I have told you, even though I was the one who lived through it. It's so hard to hold on to it. I don't want to believe it. I have not been able to sleep.

Therapist: What do you experience when you are waking up?

Ann: Afraid. My friends were telling each other their dreams but I felt I couldn't. They are too violent.

Therapist: Can you tell me?

Ann: I had this dream that feels like a flashback of a dream I have had often. I was running from these bad guys who wanted to kill me. I was on a raft in a river with this guy Jack who I wanted to have sex with, but he was paying attention to another woman, and I was upset, but then it turns out he was interested in me. We had sex and I felt like I was a whore for wanting it. These same bad guys got one guy and were mutilating his body. My dream is filled with sex being bad and me being a whore, and the world being so dangerous. How can I have a relationship if being with someone just brings up all these horrors? It's too hard to walk out in the world with all that being true. [She cries]

Faced with Ann's chronic self-doubt, I wanted her to make up her mind and end the confusion. I felt that if she would stop moving back and forth I might be able to find a comfortable place to put this experience. The media were filled with controversy about repressed-memory cases that were dismissed in court. These stories impinged on the treatment. Ann's friends questioned her treatment, in part because of these stories. She would periodically come in enraged, after seeing a newspaper article or a TV show in which people questioned the reality of sexual abuse. She feared that I might feel social pressure to question the veracity of her reports and abandon her. On rare occasions, she would feel I had some vested interest in her abuse. This was a frightening thought for her. In addition, it was a terrible thought for me that I could have put her through such pain for nothing. At other moments, she would accuse me of torturing her by encouraging her to explore her feelings and sensations, which led to more pain. A few times she changed her mind about the abuse and expected me to agree with her. I found myself whipsawed back and forth. Other times she would blame me for following her oscillations: if I was such a skillful therapist I should know and tell her the truth. I felt bad for being unable to tell her definitively what happened in her childhood. We discovered that these accusations were ways of expressing her anger and pain.

I would seek comfort by telling myself that there was a deeper issue. Ann needed to feel and demonstrate repeatedly that this was her own reality. She needed to be able to change her mind and explore her new stance, with me by her side. Ann tested concretely that I was not forcing my reality on to her and that it was truly her ideas and choice. She needed to feel that I valued her, confusion and all.

The therapist's own sense of reality can feel challenged by this process. Here is an example of a dream of mine from this period: A woman dies. Her ghost haunts her apartment. I am able to time travel and change some things. Other people think I am crazy.

Watching Ann relive her pain, I felt at times as if she was dying in front of me. This was hard for me to watch. Her daily life was haunted by traumas, so I felt I had to go back with her and explore them, even though I too would have liked to avoid them. I also felt in danger of others thinking I was crazy for believing her and working with her in this way. The voice of one instructor haunted me. Upon hearing about this patient, he said, "This patient is not analyzable." Were Ann's accusations and chronic self-doubting proof of this? I had my own self-doubts, which I had to learn how to manage. There were countercurrents to my relief. I felt proud I could help her repair some of the damage by reliving these experiences in a supportive environment. In addition, her symptoms had reduced and her sense of power and well-being had increased.

In summary, the material of severely sexually abused and traumatized patients provokes countertransference. Therapists who work with these patients need to manage feelings of helplessness, anger, sexual arousal, and flooding, or the treatment process will be derailed. The obsession with verifying the reality of the abuse or trauma is only one manifestation of chronic self-doubt. It can be restated as a question: Can I see myself as a center of thought and ideas that can exist and be held as valuable and trustworthy? This question fits both the patient and, many times, the therapist in the midst of this process as well. The issue of the "reality" of reports of abuse is discussed further in Chapter 16.

CHAPTER 11

Am I Lovable? Feeling Deep Love and Bonding

Many aspects of the damage people sustain from trauma can be summarized as feeling unloved, unlovable, or not deserving of being related to as a valuable person. People develop their core self-concept in the mirror of their parents' eyes and actions. Fraiberg's (1959) book *The Magic Years* captures children's egocentric thinking. They think the sun rises in the morning because they get up, and sets at night because they go to sleep. In trauma and abuse they think they have been mistreated because that is what they deserve, that they are in essence bad, that they caused the trauma and it is their own fault. Being abused as children leads them to see themselves as people who should be abused. This is enacted throughout their lives.

Sinason (1992) writes of the child taking in the abuse and trauma, and acting it out on deep levels. Many times children, and adults, feel compelled to conform to the powerful other's image of them communicated in words and actions. The author illustrates how many children are hated for their needs and how parents and others can wish the child dead. She demonstrates how children live this out in repetitive enactments of trying to kill themselves in large and small concrete ways. She describes cases where children deform their own bodies and minds to conform to the images and reactions of caregivers and others. She cites research evidence and case examples of how some learning disabilities are the result of child abuse and children giving up parts of their mind.

Hamilton (1989) describes how survivors organize their psychic experience around the trauma. Terr (1990, 1991) documents the concrete events of the trauma the survivor relives in repetitive memories, dreams, behaviors, and fears.

These shaping influences can mold and change the person who has experienced trauma. This all needs to be reworked in treatment.

Many sexually abused and traumatized patients have not experienced love, because of basic neglect and invalidation, or because they have had their feelings of connection ruptured. Usually some corrective process is necessary to rekindle the sense of connection, of being loved and respected. Providing reconnection can be one of the most gratifying but also frustrating tasks in treatment.

Stolorow (1986) describes the need for continuous connection to, and selfobject functions from, such patients' therapists:

> With regard to the mode of acquiring needed selfobject functions, in the more archaic states such modes ordinarily require experiences of merger or oneness with the object, together with an illusion of more or less continuous union. Hence, intrusions of the object's separateness or disruptions in the continuity of the bond can have a profoundly disintegrative impact on the subject's psychological organization . . . . It seems apparent that . . . attuned provision of requisite selfobject functions contributes vitally to the formation of psychological structure. [p. 277]

These patients need a sense of continuous connection, because they experience their emotional well-being as totally dependent on the maintenance of the connection to the therapist. Stolorow and colleagues (1987) called this belief the activation of the archaic idealizing transference.

The intensity of this connection has made me feel as though I were rocking these patients in my arms, even though I was not touching them. At other moments, I have felt like an adoptive parent. The patient's desire for continuous connection can cause the therapist to feel engulfed.

Many patients feel that they do not really exist unless therapists keep them alive in their thoughts. Patients may provoke therapists to think about them outside the session (Bromberg 1994). It is as if they need therapists to incubate them until they can be born into the larger world.

Patients seek inner cohesion and serenity, which therapists try to foster with enactments of caring. This can be helpful, but focusing on enacting care can distract from the exploration of the underlying processes that prevented patients from developing greater cohesion in the long term. The need for care is fueled by patients' convictions of worthlessness. Without exploring these underlying dynamics, patients cannot move beyond escalating enactments of caring to repair their convictions. This is because the underlying dynamic of feeling unlovable and bad is negating the long-term impact of the enactment of caring. Ultimately, without deeper exploration, therapists may become exhausted and angry trying to fill the patients' void.

Inherent in this feeling is the longing to be loved and the fantasy of recapturing the lost childhood. Even though the lost childhood can never be reclaimed, the patient needs some feelings of being loved and connected to the therapist in a way that allows the patient to psychically integrate. This fantasy is one of the most powerful desires patients bring to treatment. Many patients' enactments can be fueled by the hope to recapture their lost childhood. It can tap the therapist's deep desire to repair the patient and pull the therapist into hoping he or she can become the good parent. This mutual longing can result in each developing unrealistic hopes, expectations, and promises. This can be in the service of avoiding the intense pain of the lost childhood, and the process of acknowledging that loss and the unfeasibility (fantasy) of recapturing the childhood and life that could have been. Many times it is in this coming to terms that patients can become suicidal, not being able to face what happened, the missed possibilities, and the present circumstances of their lives. Adults in treatment may enact many young feelings in the transference, but they are still adults and need to be treated as such. Therapists need to remember that, though influential in changing the future, they cannot change the past.

It is difficult to assess exactly what these patients need from therapists, what they need from others, and what they can do for themselves. It takes time to assess what boundaries are necessary for these patients to feel safe from intrusion, and what direct interventions and enactments are necessary. I realized that I was sometimes interchanging patients' need for affection with their need for a sense of connection and safety. Therapists' enactments could have as one of their underlying motivations their desire to stop listening to the patient's pain by distracting the patient to talk about his or her good feelings toward the therapist.

Ann's treatment illustrates this need for continuous connection and feelings of love. This material also illustrates the ingenuity of patients in generating what they need.

> During the first year of treatment, when I would enter the waiting room, Ann would beam with joy; the first words she would utter were, "I was afraid you wouldn't be here." After a while, I commented on the joy in her face, which was gratifying to me. I am sensitive to others being happy to see me, because in my childhood I felt unnoticed. I interpreted how Ann felt that her emotional existence had come to depend on me to help her with her fears and memories. Ann told me, first hesitantly and then with joy, "You are now my family," and "I want to move in with you." I saw these statements as indicators of the merger transference wish or the successful establishment of the first stage of treatment. Other times I would take them more concretely, but I had mixed feelings about them. I wondered how it would be to have her move in, and realized that I did not want her to do so. I like living with my wife and children. I would feel even more subservient to her needs if I were available to her twenty-four hours a day. I feared being engulfed. Yet the idea of connection to her was appealing to me.
>
> Each improvement of Ann's connection to me would result in the re-emergence of painful memories (many of which were new memories, or more details of the traumas she had already remembered). Her good

experiences with me were precious to her, and increased her ability to face the past. This increased connection also aggravated her fear that the past would repeat itself in our relationship. I was proud of her exploration, and at the same time I dreaded it. She was gradually acquiring improved self-esteem and functioning in her daily life. These behavioral improvements were simultaneous with a reduction in her fatigue and bodily paralysis; her skin cleared up; she lost excess weight and resumed her menstrual periods after a two-year hiatus. These gains made me feel effective and more confident in the process: perhaps all the pain she endured in therapy was worthwhile.

During one period of reliving memories, she felt tremendously exposed to both the dangerous external and intrapsychic worlds. As my ten-day summer vacation approached, her fears of abandonment erupted. To hold on to me, her "little Jane" personality threatened to throw my dollhouse through the office window; and, unconsciously, Ann also began to wear revealing clothes and be seductive. When I commented on this, she was very embarrassed and ashamed, as if I were calling her a slut the way her mother would. We explored how she was trying to hold on to me the way her father demanded attention, with the offering of sexual favors. I must admit, with some shame, that part of me enjoyed the flattery.

Over time, she showed signs of internalizing the treatment. These internalizations were part of the developing positive transference and identification process, and were not a defensive avoidance. She was able to create connected experiences with me as a good parent. She wished I would take her to the movies and buy her popcorn. We explored her wishes and hopes that I would like her, her feeling close to me, and her romantic feelings. She was then able to go to the movies for the first time in many years. She told me that she felt that I was with her, and that she had a wonderful time. We explored her wishes for what she wanted from her father, and her sadness when this did not occur. This set of experiences reinforced a concept of treatment about which I had been uncertain. That patients need open space, contained but unintruded upon by the therapist, to explore feelings and fantasies, and less concrete enactments than I had originally thought. In an accepting environment, patients will often create the rest of the experience they

need. Ann created for herself an internalization, as well as an enactment of the curative union fantasy.

In another instance, Ann told me she wished to marry me. She said
that she wanted me to hold her and have sex with her. Exploring this
imagery, it became apparent that while she really wanted to be close
and feel my love, she did not feel old enough to have sex. She closed
her eyes and imagined me kissing her; she told me all of the sensations in her body, feeling her body unite and melt into mine. She said
that this was one of the most wonderful experiences she had had. I was
gratified. Later, she told me that she felt like a virgin again. Upon further analysis, this meant that the union of bodies had repaired the damaging experiences of her childhood and she no longer felt dirty. I responded that she was a virgin to good relationships (I responded to the
hoped-for cure on the same fantasized level). She beamed. I felt happy
for her, and relieved of the pressure to have physical contact with her.
At the same time I felt a little sad. Part of me had enjoyed her fantasy of
marrying me, which had made me feel attractive and younger.

Ann's treatment illustrates the benefit of giving patients the space
to have their own experience. Most therapists misunderstand and feel
anxious when a patient experiences and communicates intense emotion, traumatic experience, or body experience; often the therapist
will foreclose these experiences (e.g., by interrupting) to protect
against such anxiety. Speaking to patients during such experiences
can interrupt the process. Therapists must wait and contain themselves while patients are involved with the experience. Only later
can patients be open to describing and co-creating a narrative of the
experience with the therapist. Many therapists move in too quickly,
and do not allow the experience to flower. What the experience
means to patients may be different from what therapists presuppose.
Therapists may need to ask patients the meaning of the experience
before putting forth their own structure. At times therapists need
to encourage patients to move deeply and to explore the associations,
meanings, and sensations. Different patients are attuned to different
sensations.

As in the example above, a patient can live out new experiences
with the therapist helping to internalize a sense of worth. Some more

concrete representation of the continuous caring and connection may be necessary. Even then the therapist does not have to provide it directly but can use symbolic objects or experiences. Transitional objects can facilitate internalization.

> During a period when Celeste was in a state of terror, regularly making late-night calls to tell me about her suicidal impulses, she asked for a piece of my clothing. I gave her a sweater, which she wore when feeling fearful. The sweater made her feel cared for because I had listened and responded to her request. When she wore it she felt heard, safer, and connected. The late-night calls occurred less frequently. I have given other patients rocks, shells, pictures, or audiotapes of soothing messages designed for them.
>
> To have deeper connections with these patients is demanding but may be required to help them. This kind of treatment is in part a lifestyle choice for therapists. The maintenance of the connection involves many powerful feelings and dramas. A deeper understanding of these makes unconscious and destructive enactments less likely.
>
> My tolerance for this demanding process was enhanced by my identification with my mother, whom I idealized as the educated caregiver and "supernurse." Sometimes I would wait up for her when she would get home late from her work at the hospital. She would tell me how she had cared for her patients. She showed great concern for their emotional needs. This experience, too, shaped my career choice. I wanted to be more like my explosive but caring mother than my distant, violent father.
>
> These patients also fit my style because of my own abandonment issues. Once these patients become fully attached, they rarely leave; treatment is often lengthy. There is also an early transference, in which patients experience deep love for therapists. This was also gratifying to my need for love.

In summary, patients need a sense of being cared about, and taken care of, by therapists. Enactments of caring by therapists can help, but by themselves can increase patients' demands. Sometimes patients demand a demonstration that they are lovable, and make requests for special treatment such as physical demonstrations of love, reduced fees, or excessive phone conversations. In more extreme cases, patients ask therapists for cohabitation, physical contact, or even sex. Therapists may try to answer the demands with special favors. There needs to be a balance between two necessary processes, caregiving and exploration.

Inexperienced therapists usually feel comfortable caring, but not with the pain of exploring trauma. They need to understand patients' enactments as potential openings to deeper experience. If patients are to be helped, they need to explore and recognize the pain of what happened to them, and examine how they have internalized their abuse as indicative of their worth. To support permanent change, patients need to understand how these negative internalizations prevent them from experiencing connection with others and with others' care.

CHAPTER 12

Can You See Me? Discontinuous and Shattered Existence

Janet, Breuer, and Ferenczi all used the concept of dissociation in their writings on traumatized and sexually abused patients (see Chapter 1). Currently the controversy over the place of dissociation in the field of psychoanalysis continues, especially in relation to trauma and sexual abuse survivors. Davies and Frawley (1992a, 1994) see dissociation as the hallmark of having been sexually abused. They define dissociation as follows:

> Dissociation is the process of severing connections between categories of mental events—between events that seem irreconcilably different, between the actual events and their affective and emotional significance, between actual events and the awareness of their cognitive significance, and finally, as in the case of severe trauma, between the actual occurrence of real events and their permanent, symbolic, verbal mental representation . . . . Traditionally, then, dissociation is defined as a process by which a piece of traumatic experience, because it is too overstimulating to be processed and recorded along the usual channels, is cordoned off and established as a separate psychic state within the personality, creating two (or more) ego states that alternate in consciousness and, under different internal and ex-

ternal circumstances, emerge to think, behave, remember, and feel.
[Davies and Frawley 1994, pp. 62–63]

Davies and Frawley see the relationship between sexual abuse and dissociation as cause and effect: if you have been sexually abused, you will have dissociation as a major coping strategy. They have delineated patterns of "alters," or dissociated states, and the relationships between them (Davies and Frawley 1992a). Davies and Frawley believe that these dissociated states or alter personalities need to be spoken to directly as separate persons who have critical knowledge and experiences unavailable to other parts of the person.

Shengold (1992) considers Davies and Frawley's views on the use of dissociation by sexually abused patients as overly simplistic and missing the important individuality of each patient. He asserts that there are many traumatized and sexually abused patients who do not dissociate and instead use other defenses. He views Davies and Frawley's approach of addressing the parts as misguided.

Davies and Frawley (1992b) view Shengold and other traditional analysts as not noticing sexual-abuse material or dissociative disorders because there are characteristics of the classical psychoanalytic technique (e.g., abstinence) that make these patients fearful, and they therefore will not show the regressed aspects or personalities; the protector personality may be the only one who speaks in sessions. These patients may stay in analysis because of compliance, attachment, or fear. Ferenczi (1933) also made reference to the regressed aspects of a person not emerging when the analyst takes an abstinent stance.

Another view is expressed by Bromberg (1994), who applies dissociation broadly in that he sees all people dissociating to some degree. In this conception, traumatic dissociation is just a more extreme version of normal coping.

Some attempts have been made to describe the symptoms of traumatic experience with bioneurological models or metaphors of brain function. These metaphors can be instructive for the psychotherapist if they are not reified. Curtis (1993) has developed a dissociation model of the mind. She sees the mind as a system of modular functions that, under stress, lose their interconnections and become dissociated. Grigsby and colleagues (1991) summarize brain research that supports this model as well.

Methods of surviving trauma are influenced by memory encoding, storage, and retrieval, and are seen by some authors as explaining dissociation. Clyman (1992) and other researchers (e.g., Herman 1992) emphasize the existence of three types of memory: procedural (bodily/kinesthetic), declarative (verbal/linguistic), and traumatic (unprocessed sensory/flashback). These will be discussed further in Chapter 16. Some of these different methods of encoding and retrieval have implications for the way treatment is conducted and the way symptoms may manifest themselves.

Like Ferenczi (1933), I believe fright and even mild trauma create some dissociation. Each person's mind may react differently. How minds shatter and try to mend themselves after extreme trauma can make for idiosyncratic structuring of experience. If sufficiently intense, trauma and abuse can shatter one's sense of a unified self. Such experiences can lead one to feel that other people and even existence itself are too dangerous. Certain traumatic events are too intense to be experienced directly, so part of the person dies or separates off, as a means of survival and protection. In the shattering experience of trauma, psychic walls can be destroyed, weakening boundaries between internal and external experience. Victims then can build new walls to separate, hide, and shield themselves from other people, and against parts of themselves. The intensity of the trauma may lead victims to believe that it happened to someone else, that they do not exist, or that a new person has been born in their place. They may feel that the experience is separated, so that those moments don't seem real, or are experienced in a disembodied way, as if the patient were watching it happen on television. The extent of support for victims after the trauma heavily determines the trauma's lasting effects.

This process of separation has been described by different words (e.g., "dissociation," "splitting," "double consciousness," etc.); I use "dissociation." Dissociation manifests itself on a continuum, from mild to severe. I can see glimpses of it in most people, as Bromberg maintains, for example when one is driving a car and loses track of time. Dissociation in its more severe forms undermines our assumption of the unitary nature of the self. There can be a resistance to viewing people as discontinuous. The concept of dissociation implies that people's experiences of themselves are not uniform, that experience can shift from moment to moment. What we think of as ourselves, our history, our place in the world, and our relationships can shift rapidly. This can raise anxiety because other people are critical to our lives.

These dissociated states emerge in a patient during sessions. If welcomed, the therapeutic relationship can utilize moments of dissociation to explore the patient's other states of being. These moments can be recognized in the patient's voice, behavior, and mannerisms, which may become different and often much younger. Therapists can welcome these states, connecting with patients during them as if they are speaking to younger people. Even in the average neurotic patient, openings such as these will emerge. Words that are often repeated by patients can be explored for their meaning and associations. Therapists can explore patients' body sensations, such as images, sounds, and smells. These moments and sensations can be keys to open the patient's deeper, more dissociated experiences, which may allow access to memories not available in other states of being.

The connection between dissociation and sexual abuse is made by many authors but most powerfully by Davies and Frawley (1992a, 1994). Severe sexual abuse with violence has been linked strongly to multiple personality disorder by many researchers, especially Putnam (1989) and Loewenstein and Ross (1992).

The first time I recognized that a patient of mine (Celeste) was manifesting more-than-transient dissociative states in session with me, it involved the emergence of a complete multiple personality.

In my clinical experience Celeste was a twin or precursor of Ann. As I have described earlier, when Celeste came into treatment she had had numerous but unavailing medical procedures, including a hysterectomy, to relieve her chronic vaginal pain. She had then entered body-massage therapy, where she started having memories. The therapist felt these memories were out of his realm, and he referred her to me. She had memories of abuse by her father that included his use of a vise and other tools to stretch and crush her genitals. She then remembered that he sold her to other men for money to use her in any way they wished. I felt angry at him. It was hard to listen to these accounts.

I explored my feelings about her material in my analysis and supervision. She talked of surviving these events by leaving her body and visiting the angels who helped her. Then she remembered her mother being beaten and raped by her father, and by other men with her father's consent.

Celeste would call late at night, threatening to kill herself. These became regular, night-long dramas. For months I rarely slept. I was always tired. I had nightmares. Often I would be torn up, thinking, Please don't die; I couldn't live with the guilt. Though worn down, I avoided vacations because her feelings of abandonment increased her suicidal feelings. If I took vacations, I would conduct sessions over pay phones by the side of the road. I remember many dinners at restaurants with my family where I was on the phone with Celeste trying to convince her not to kill herself. Somehow, I had come to feel as though my existence depended on Celeste's not killing herself. I would bring my feelings in to my supervision and analysis.

I struggled with Celeste's eloquent pleas to be physically held, and with my feeling inadequate to meet her needs. We explored her longings and her experience of a hug. I agreed that she needed the touch because it made her feel more integrated; I was convinced, however, that I could not hold her and explore her sexual material and still maintain a therapeutic stance. I told her that I could not do it, partly because of my being a man and her a woman. On her own, she eventually started seeing a female therapist concurrently, who would hold her. She found that this arrangement greatly helped her tolerate the more painful affect and feel whole.

When Celeste proposed needing to be held and possibly seeing another therapist, I was fearful of losing her. But I also felt relief. The depth of my attachment to Celeste, as with Ann, shocked me. It was as if Ann and Celeste had become like the daughters I had never had (I have two sons). Six to seven sessions a week at reasonable fees also made the financial aspect feel real. I was grateful to have another therapist take over some of the responsibility and serve as my backup during emergencies and vacations. I never spoke with the other therapist, whom I believe Celeste saw once or twice a week. I gave up trying to control the treatment and followed Celeste's lead. I felt crucial to the process, but it had a life of its own.

After Celeste had spent about a year with me and the other therapist, a personality emerged of a 4-year-old girl who called herself Mary. Celeste, the host personality, said that her other therapist had told her she was a "multiple." Mary remembered many previously unknown events from childhood. These specific events will be discussed in a later chapter.

Celeste believed that by holding her, the other therapist had allowed younger ego states to emerge. I wondered if some "personalities" would interpret the holding the way it was intended, while others would misinterpret it as a sexual threat.

When Celeste experienced me as not believing she had multiple personalities, she would in essence say, "I have another therapist who does. If you don't get with the program, you are history."

This experience with Celeste challenged many of my assumptions about human functioning. I found myself questioning the reality of the phenomenon of multiple personalities. Could these child personas be experienced by the patient as who they are in that moment without a feeling of really being an adult? Even during session I wondered whether the patient could be pretending in some sense. I had heard about such behavior and had colleagues who had treated it, but it was different to face it myself. My patient was adamant and felt insulted by this questioning. She reported not knowing things in the child personality that she knew in the adult personality, and vice versa. The child personalities seemed frozen in time in the childhood traumatic states. With each personality, it was like starting therapy over, with a person of a different age, and style. I had to develop a new therapeutic alliance. These new, usually traumatized, persons of different ages and developmental levels had to be brought through their own specific constellations of traumas from their own perspective. I had to learn to talk directly to the specific "person" while realizing that some other personalities might be listening in. It was like doing individual therapy with other family members listening or dropping in, with all the constituent conflicts. Over time I began to feel more comfortable with the situation and to believe in its reality.

Then a situation occurred with Ann to reinforce my experiences with Celeste.

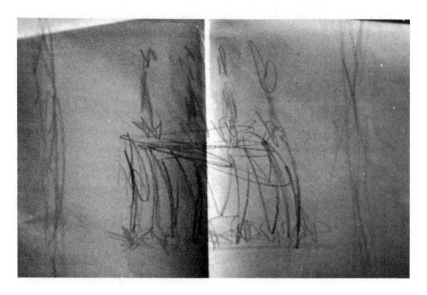

Figure 12-1

I had been seeing Ann for over four years, four to five times per week. Usually she would lie on the couch. In one session she sat up and her head dropped to her chest. She groaned, and a little squeaky voice came out. She got up from the couch, and started hopping around the room like a little girl. Ann had never behaved this way. Her squeaky voice said, "I'm Jessie." Jessie told me that, after seeing a book on multiple personalities, she was angry at me for not recognizing her and forcing her to hide. As she was talking, she was playing with my toy dolls. She told me that she had come out earlier, but that I had told her to go away. When I asked her how I had done so, she said I had insisted that she was part of Ann. Jessie said, "I'm not part of Ann. Ann doesn't even know I'm here." I asked Jessie how old she was, and she said 6. Ann is a skilled artist who is right-handed. When Jessie started drawing, however, she drew a birthday cake as a 6-year-old would, and with her left hand. The cake she drew is in Figure 12-1.

I wondered out loud what made her feel comfortable coming out at this moment. She told me that she had come out because I had said she was always welcome. I had thought that I was doing "inner child" work, encouraging the patient to express deep childhood needs. She then told me that seeing the book on multiple personalities in the hand of another patient made her brave enough to come out.

I wondered, had the book put the idea in her head, or had I? Jessie's personality structure felt different from Ann's, with past and present memories that only partly overlapped. I had experience with Celeste coming out as a multiple, but the phenomenon was still new and uncertain to me. As my acceptance of Jessie and the existence of multiple personalities firmed, so did Jessie's trust in me. As her trust grew, five or six other personalities quickly emerged. My experience with each personality and its own differences and memories confirmed my belief in multiple personality disorder.

At other times, I wondered if by some contagion Ann had picked up the multiple personality disorder from Celeste in the waiting room. As far as I knew, the two had only said hello. Yet it was Celeste's book that Ann had seen in the waiting room. Ann had been seeing Celeste in the waiting room for more than a year. They both were coming at least five times per week. Ann noticed Celeste often, but Celeste hardly noticed Ann. Ann often idealized Celeste as having more education and leading the kind of life Ann might have had without the abuse. Ann fantasized Celeste's pads of paper, books, and tape recorders as indicative of supervision in a psychotherapy training program. Ann often talked of Celeste as if she were her envied older sister. Ann had cut off contact with her own older sister, who would not believe the abuse even though Ann remembered her sister having also been abused.

Little did Ann know that Celeste, although financially better off and married, was not better educated or more functional. She brought notebooks and tape recorders because she had trouble holding on to the memories that were emerging. A year later, after seeing Celeste in bad shape one day, Ann guessed that Celeste was coming to treatment because she was an incest survivor and probably had multiple personalities.

Ann gave me pieces of art (Figures 12–2, 12–3, and 12–4) that illustrated her inner world and her personalities. One piece, done years before treatment, showed her as a baby girl with walls inside her head. Within each wall was a depiction of an incident that we later realized was the birth of a personality: Ann being cut with a knife, molested by her father, and tortured with crosses, and most of the other memories that were recovered over the ten-year treatment.

Figure 12-2

Figures 12–2, 12–3, 12–4 illustrate her dissociation. Different realities exist side by side; they are manifested in separate states or personalities, which collaborated on these pictures while Ann remained unaware of the events they clearly depict.

Figure 12-3

Figure 12-4

She drew some of her different personalities. One little baby had a bottle and flowers (Figure 12–5). It was confusing to me to want to cuddle and coo a baby while her adult body was in front of me.

THIS IS
BABY
SUSIE
WITH
HER
BOTTLE
AND A
FLOWER
IN HER
HAIR

← FAT
TUMMY

Figure 12-5

A boy named Charlie, 4 or 5 years old, came into being when Ann's father took a gun and shoved it into her vagina, threatening to kill her (described earlier). This boy took on the name of the Vietcong her father had been trying to kill, and the emotional tone her father had assumed during the enactment. He remembered his father burning him in an oven as well. Figure 12–6 was done when Charlie first emerged. This drawing is of Charlie fighting in a war zone, and represents his feelings about the world. The next picture (Figure 12–7) is of Charlie a month later. After a month of working with his anger on an "individual" basis his anger had decreased and his world seemed safer to him.

Figure 12-6

As the separate personalities felt understood, the therapy began to change the separate parts. I had to keep track of several parallel therapies, each with its own shifting transferences, associations, and sensitivities. It was the equivalent of playing a game of three-dimensional chess that kept changing because there was some unpredictable communication between dimensions, and new dimensions would emerge. In a sense, therapy had to start over every time a new part appeared. Each part progressed somewhat separately in individual therapy, with some conjoint therapy or "family work."

Another personality was a scared 3-year-old girl, shown in the left-hand side of Figure 12–8. If I moved or even breathed she would disappear. It took months to develop a relationship with her. Another personality was a young college-age adult. On the right-hand side of Figure 12–8, a younger part, Sarah, is writing about the older part, Kathryn.

CHARLIE

CHARLIE
FISHES + FIGHTS
AND HE'S
MAD AND
SAD AND
DOESN'T
LIKE TO
TALK
TO ME,

Figure 12-7

Figure 12–9 depicts one of the personalities, Sarah. She yearned to be close to me and have me protect her so she could feel strong and safe. This picture helped her live out the fantasies in her mind. She benefited from telling me about it in detail without my physically doing what she fantasized. She imagined two of us going to the beach together, having fun swimming and playing in the sand. She imagined feeling safe, protected, and expansive. This was a step in her ability to feel these feelings in the outer world.

There were adolescent personalities who liked to rebel and use drugs. These personalities refused to come to session; they would sabotage treatment and sometimes Ann's jobs, which they thought were a drag. Only after negotiation with them did treatment settle down.

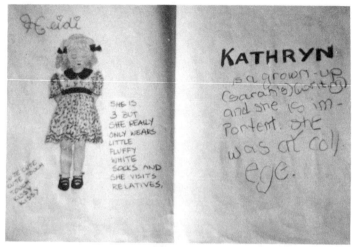

Figure 12-8

Figure 12-9

For example, if they allowed Ann to go to work and therapy, then she would buy them rollerblades and allow time for drug use. These adolescent personalities were both male and female. The girls fought hard to date men and have sex. This was a complex negotiation.

"Jessie" told me how I had suppressed her "selves" by my inability to take in their presence. I realized retrospectively that different personalities had been switching in and out for years. Ann and I had colluded to ignore many cues. Ann recalled throwing her diaries away because other people kept making entries; she recalled lost time periods, occasions of different body posture, and voice changes. Years later in treatment, Ann told me her greatest hurt in analysis was that I pushed "Jessie" away for so long.

What increased my belief in dissociative disorders was reading more widely. Recently, in the area of sexual abuse treatment, the dissociation model has been resurrected. I have found support for my views on dissociation and multiple personalities in articles by Davies and Frawley in *Psychoanalytic Dialogues* (1992a,b), as well as by Loewenstein and Ross in *Psychoanalytic Inquiry* (1992).

Recognition of the dissociative process, especially its extreme forms, establishes a different relationship between therapists and patients. Therapists need to be sensitized to separate states of being that can exist simultaneously. These states can also be in conflict. Many times one state of being is desperate for treatment while another opposes it. Some personalities and interactions between personalities can be known to some of the personalities, but hidden from others.

The next patient is a composite of many whose treatment I have supervised; for the purposes of this composite (including discussions of countertransference issues) the therapist is female. This composite illustrates the interactions and enactments as they were experienced by the therapist with the emergence of dissociated self states. It illustrates some initial problems in dealing with different parts. First, the parts are usually filled with painful affects that need to be contained and processed. The parts need to be recognized, and treated as having different needs and agendas. A therapeutic alliance needs to be secured with each part, or that part will feel ignored or antagonistic and potentially sabotage the treatment.

A trauma's impact on the therapist is part of what Pearlman and Saakvitne (1995) call vicarious traumatization. The following situation illustrates how directly traumatic this work can be.

The adult patient was referred by another therapist who found treating her to be too stressful. It emerged that the patient's father tortured and sexually abused her as a child. She felt sure he intended to kill her, and at times she wished to die. The patient reenacted these events as an adult through self-destructive thoughts and actions—cutting herself, walking at night on freeways, and having sex with strangers.

The therapist had encountered some childlike aspects of this patient. This patient had told the therapist how much she loved her but couldn't believe the therapist cared about her.

Months into treatment, this normally tense patient came in seeming calm. The therapist felt unsettled by this unexplained change and asked, "What's going on? You seem so calm." The patient handed the therapist a piece of paper, on which was written, "I'll kill this sniveling bitch!"

The therapist was shocked. Finally, she asked, "Who wrote this?" The patient shifted in affect and style, and said, "I'll kill this stupid bitch because she believes your therapist drivel."

The parental part, which was male, wanted to kill the child part, which wanted to connect to the therapist. The therapist realized, or wished to believe, that the adult was trying to protect the child from hurt and betrayal by the therapist, which would be an injury worse than death.

Trying to connect with the killer part without endangering the patient was difficult. The killer part felt that he could kill off the child part yet live himself. He assumed that there were two bodies and not one. He enjoyed the idea of killing the child part and inflicting pain. This killer part was identified with the sadistic father. These discussions went on for months.

Finally the killer part said, "She will never learn, so I just have to exterminate her like a roach!"

The therapist responded: "If we work together on an outpatient basis, we must have an agreement to protect everyone from getting hurt."

"No!" said the killer.

The therapist found herself shaken. She asked if the patient wanted to be hospitalized; the patient refused, saying, "The hospital is worse than death, and what makes you think I cannot kill myself there?"

The therapist felt powerless and could not reach the patient. But at least with the patient in the hospital, the therapist felt comforted that "I had done what I could and it was the hospital's responsibility."

The therapist ruminated silently, How am I going to make contact with this patient? Don't kill yourself. I have become so attached to you. I have come to care about you. I don't know if I could live with myself if you were to kill yourself. I can't take your daily suicide threats. They're too stressful. It's as if the killer part was torturing not just the child part but me, too. I want to kill the one who wants to kill.

This therapist had believed that in therapy, the therapist could count on transference and attachment to get through the hard times. Because of this patient's disconnection, she felt powerless. What surprised her was the intensity of her anger toward the patient. She thought, this is some kind of enactment, and I don't want to be part of it.

Talking to the host personality, the therapist said the patient had to promise to protect herself or she had to be hospitalized. The patient stated, "I'm not going to the hospital."

The therapist replied, "Then we have to contact someone who will stay with you for a few days."

The patient initially refused but the therapist told her she would have to call the police. Then the patient agreed. Since the patient lived alone, the plan was that an informed person would accompany her twenty-four hours a day for the next few days. The patient was very angry about this arrangement. She felt that the therapist had taken away her only escape from life.

The killer part and the therapist started developing a therapeutic alliance. The killer part needed to feel he was getting something out of treatment, including smoking dope, sex, and control of treatment. They began working through the killer part's feelings of disconnection; in time he no longer felt the need to kill.

> After this experience, the therapist vigilantly watched for the next trauma, fearful of any sign that the patient might act out again. The therapist was traumatized, and for a long time she was very fearful of being emotionally traumatized again in her work with this and her other patients. This fear interfered with her normally excellent empathic abilities.

This example makes apparent the agony of the therapist. The therapist's experience was directly traumatic in the assaultiveness of direct threats and in feeling helpless to stop the suicide attempts. The therapist experienced increased fearfulness and terror generated by this patient's suicidal enactments, which could easily be retriggered by other patients. It was also vicariously traumatic through being empathically immersed, while this patient was reexperiencing the intense pain and desperation of the original trauma and its internalized dynamics within the patient.

This vignette also illustrates the importance of being aware of the parts of the patient's personality, and of enlisting the sabotaging parts into the treatment process. All the parts have important talents and feelings to contribute to the functioning of the person.

The difficulty in treating patients' sadistic, angry, and fearful alter personalities is discussed below by Charles Olsen, M.D., who has graciously given me permission to present his experiences. Dr. Olsen is an eminent psychiatrist, a founding member of the Institute of Contemporary Psychotherapy in Washington, DC, and a faculty member of the Washington Psychoanalytic Society. Here is an excerpt from his publicly delivered invited discussion of a paper I presented at the 1997 Annual Convention of the Self in Washington, DC.

> If this can be understood in some fundamental way, then it will be easy to accept Dr. Perlman's fundamental point that: "What the patient needs most from the therapist is for the therapist to feed back an understanding of the patient's intense fear of being hurt again and her desperate hope for help." That is, from the same therapist she hopes will help her, [the patient] fears the hurt. A multiple of mine had a six-inch-in-diameter, ulcerating sore on her left hip. She kept

picking at it to keep it ulcerating, much to the distress of several other alters and myself. She wanted me to look at it and minister to it and I declined and sent her to an internist. Ultimately I was able to access the alter responsible. This alter quite matter-of-factly admitted to continuing the ulceration and said: "As long as she is ugly, pussy, and smelly, you won't fuck her." I said that given what I knew of her history . . . it was perfectly reasonable to be concerned about my fucking her, but had he observed over the months we had worked together any behavior on my part that would support that concern? [As] there was not, [she] subsequently let the sore heal.

It brought to mind my own form of posttraumatic stress disorder (PTSD), which I suffered as a result of vicarious traumatization and unsuspecting introjection of evil malignancies. I still do not understand exactly how or for what reason it happened. At its worst point my PTSD required lying perfectly still, flat on my back, with my ankles crossed in a quite particular way; and if I was lucky the electricity that seemed to be surging through my body would stop in about an hour and a half and I could go to sleep, dreading the early morning awakening that was soon to come. Yes, some therapists have trouble relaxing away from the office. This state resulted from my trying to work on an outpatient basis with what turned out to be a highly complex multiple who was seriously suicidal by the time she was 2½. She was the multiple from hell, you know, like the borderline from hell only fifty times worse, who, until you get your bearings, will take you down the pike every time. And try getting your bearings in this kind of situation when the only supervisor available was swamped and limited supervision to five visits. Actually, she didn't seem like the multiple from hell as I was engaged in a never-ending struggle to calm and manage many severely damaged, victimized alters. I think, off to the side, in some ways I could not comprehend, malignant persecutory/protector alters were having a heyday with my head and guts.

I was so into denial after that case, for I never wanted to encounter a multiple again, that I missed all of the signs of abuse and dissociation in my second abused patient during two years of intensive work. The most notable example came one day when she walked out of the office and casually said that she had been playing with her loaded

.357 Magnum. I said in an equally glib and casual way, "Well, be careful," and didn't think another second about it. The next morning at 4 A.M. I sat bolt upright in bed, sweating profusely and feeling stark terror as I finished a dream of her blowing her brains out all over my face, shirt, and tie. Needless to say, I hospitalized her, and diagnosed her multiplicity. With enormous sadness and guilt—for we had worked hard together to establish a nascent trust over two years of work—I transferred her to someone else, because I was not completely recovered from my PTSD of my first case.

These things are read easier than they are lived because now I have my stimulus barrier back. In the middle of my PTSD that I was trying desperately to deny, I was watching *Sleeping Beauty* with my daughter. When the wicked queen came on the scene I was filled with palpable physical revulsion, for I now had experienced that there were truly real, evil people in this world, and at that moment she represented it all for me in a most unsettling way. I finally admitted I was in deep trouble, returned to treatment, and made a rational disposition of this patient. Whoever said that the craziness usually goes away if you understand the dissociation was wrong!

Dr. Olsen's experience illustrates the impact of treating some disturbed patients. This patient wreaked havoc on the psyche of this therapist, but she also probably tapped into some unresolved issues in Dr. Olsen.

In contrast to Dr. Olsen's brave engagement of the dissociated parts, if the therapist does not delve into these other states of being, treatment may not progress beyond a superficial adaptation. From this perspective, therapists may be speaking mostly to the host personality, which may not feel truly alive. This is reminiscent of Winnicott's (1972b) true/false dichotomy. Winnicott stated that the therapist's lack of awareness may result in treating the false persona. When this occurs, there will be little change and increase in "aliveness" because so much of the person remains untouched.

Should the treatment strive for the full integration of the personalities into one personality? Multiple personality structure may have some advantages. For example, Ann could swim well. As one personality became tired another would come out and feel fresh, able to race and swim farther. Based on this example, a more limited integration with increased voluntary utilization of the dissociation could be supported as an alternate goal.

Ever since my experiences with Ann and Celeste, I feel changed. Whenever I hear patients say, "I felt like a different person" or "I never felt the same since," I wonder what exactly they are saying. When people are flaky, seem disoriented, forget a lot, or have blackouts, I look for evidence of dissociation, including more severe dissociative disorders. When patients cannot remember periods of their childhood, I look for the possibility that another personality can. I might ask, "Is there anyone else inside you who might know?" I watch for posture and voice-quality changes as indicators of possible switching.

The difficulty with multiple personality disorder, as with many aspects of the field of trauma and sexual abuse, is the feeling of uncertainty. Could this phenomenon be "enacted" rather than "real"? This thought, though rare, does occasionally pass through my mind, although, in general, I am a firm believer in the phenomenon.

CHAPTER 13

Who Is Bad and Who Is the Abuser?

I started to listen to my patients when, in their attacks, they called me insensitive, cold, even hard and cruel; when they reproached me with being selfish, heartless, conceited; when they shouted at me, "Help! Quick! Don't let me perish helplessly!" Then I began to test my conscience in order to discover whether, despite all my conscious good intentions, there might after all be some truth in these accusations. [Ferenczi 1933, p. 157]

"Knife! Blood! [Silent scream] You murdered me!"
[Sexual abuse survivor, to her therapist]
"I'm not the one who murdered you! I'm trying to help you! Stop messing with my mind!" [Therapist]

Patients who have suffered abuse have usually internalized the tragedies in their lives on many levels. In Chapter 11, the internalized senses of being bad and unlovable were explicated. The present chapter describes other levels at which the trauma is internalized and acted out in relationships, and the resulting transferences and countertransferences.

IN RELATIONSHIPS

In daily life each person must set limits with others. This ability can often be lacking in abused patients due to their experience. To survive the abuse and pain, these patients have had to deactivate their normal alarm systems and protest behaviors. This sets up a likelihood of not being able to stop mistreatment in adulthood, even when it is detected, because they have learned to not respond or act on their feelings. These patients can then become easy targets for further exploitation.

In a more active form, these tragedies are enacted repetitively as Davies and Frawley (1992a, 1994), and Herman (1992) highlight. Hamilton (1989) describes how trauma becomes a psychic organizer of all experience.

IN TREATMENT

Patients can experience common therapeutic practices as enactments of abuse. The patients and therapists may feel assaulted by each other's pain, needs, and demands. Patients may experience therapists as abusers who are forcing them to reexperience the pain. Therapists, in turn, may feel helpless in their role, as they are forced to listen to the flood of affect and deal with what it stimulates within them.

The treatment process is one in which the toxins that this traumatized person has psychically ingested are encouraged to be brought into the therapy, in order to be understood and worked through. These enacted dramas are usually unconscious identifications and split off or dissociated and encapsulated traumas. To be fully reintegrated into the person, the traumas need to be allowed to emerge in whatever form is accessible. This is usually a raw, unprocessed action. It often takes an intense experience to break open the barriers of the walled-off separation and allow the trauma to be experienced consciously. Then these more procedurally encoded traumatic memories can be constructively reexamined and worked through with words in the therapeutic process. This means that therapists may be forced into roles in the enactments—to feel panic, helplessness, rage, love, or need. Most therapists find this process a strain. Some therapists choose not to treat these patients and refer them elsewhere. Other therapists out of desperation or denial may force the patient out of treatment, or squelch exploration.

One of the most trying and yet inevitable experiences in treating abuse and trauma survivors is the negative or repetitive transference in which they experience the therapist as the perpetrator. They begin to behave and react to the therapist in a way that indicates the therapist is dangerous or has hurt them. This conflicts with most therapists' own self-image and ideal. The patient's reaction is usually based in part on some accurate detail of the therapeutic situation or the therapist's behavior (Stolorow et al. 1987). Disentangling who and what is contributing to this interaction can be a delicate and complex exploration, where timing and self-reflection are critical. Illustrating parts of this are the opening quotations to this chapter.

The preceding chapters give examples of enactments of trauma and abuse, in particular of patients who threaten suicide and traumatize the therapist. It would be interesting to explore what Dr. Olsen and his patient were enacting in the interactions described in the previous chapter.

It is common for patients who have been sexually abused and traumatized to have difficulty with finances. Money and financial power in our culture lend themselves to representing power/authority/domination because they are concrete and so widely acknowledged. Therefore, money could have significant personal meanings for abused patients not specifically related to their abuse, even when the original abuse did not involve money. As a result traumatized patients may have problems managing money because of the equivalence of money and power in our culture.

On a different level, traumatized patients may have trouble with money because money may have been an integral part of the abuse, raising issues of enactments. For example, the patient may have been sold to others or have been given money to not tell others about the abuse. Paying the therapist may evoke these feelings and meanings, possibly turning the therapist into the abuser or the abused.

Alternatively, money can also be a way of expressing entitlement and power, and patients may fear that to be powerful will provoke others to hurt them. Therefore, patients may sabotage their own financial success because it represents an assertion of themselves and a challenge to the abuser.

In these enactments there is usually an interlocking of transference and countertransference. Most patients, particularly traumatized and abused ones, have issues around money. Many of these patients wish they had been rescued from the abuse/trauma and, similarly, now wish to be rescued from their pain. With many patients I have found myself enacting a rescue of my sister from my abusive parents by allowing these patients reduced fees and exorbitant credit. I have experienced myself as the abuser for wanting these traumatized patients to pay their bill, even though with other patients it feels more routine.

I set an initial low fee with Ann and then subsequently lowered it further. Even then, she did not pay her bill for long periods and built up a large debt. Ann experienced me as the "abuser" who was forcing her to pay what she could not and, as the victim, should not have to because she had paid too much in pain in her life. In addition, she felt she should not have to pay for love that she deserved but did not get from her parents. So I, as a representative of this unfair world, should give therapy free to compensate for her past.

When I pressed the issue, another of her personalities emerged and called me a "sucker" for allowing her to pay such a low fee and running up a large debt. When she called me a "sucker," I felt enraged. I became paralyzed with fear of my intense anger and barely spoke for the rest of the session for fear of what I would say or do. Over the next weeks we explored all our feelings. Was she reversing roles and becoming the abuser? Was this a feeling she had been having for a long time but had been fearful to express?

In my analysis at that time I explored my overidentification with Ann. My survivor guilt led me to do more for her than was appropriate. What emerged for me was that when I set limits with these patients, such as asking to be paid, I would unconsciously relive my traumas on a bodily level. The experience was similar to saying no to my mother, and having my mother retaliate by hitting me with a car. In addition, I would at times either identify with my father, for whom money was a topic that would regularly trigger a violent rage, or reexperience myself as the victim of these rages with the patient in the role of my father. Both roles were unsavory for me.

There are important issues of management of money with sexually abused and traumatized patients. These patients are usually in need of long-term, intensive treatment, and are not functioning well when they come for help. Private practice is constituted such that therapists must negotiate financial arrangements at the start of treatment, with little knowledge of patients' lives. In addition, therapists must charge fees when patients' functioning often compromises their ability to produce income. Thus, therapists need to assess financial issues at the outset, or they may be caught later in a situation where the patients' money runs out. Therapists must set adequate fees or they themselves will become resentful, because these patients can be taxing. Some compromise must be reached between the therapists' needs and the patients' finances. Too much of a reduction may enact a rescue fantasy that cannot be sustained. Many therapists find that their self-image as a helper is in conflict with the necessity to make a living.

Davies and Frawley (1992a, 1994) have described eight scripts and roles that are enacted between the patient and therapist in the treatment of sexually abused patients. These transference–countertransference enactments were presented in the introduction to Part II, and include the uninvolved nonabusing parent and the neglected child; the sadistic abuser and the helpless, impotently enraged victim; the idealized, omnipotent rescuer and the entitled child who demands to be rescued; and the seducer and the seduced.

Although Davies and Frawley do not more fully acknowledge the individuality of the patient, they usefully alert us to dramas often enacted by sexually abused patients. These roles frequently reverse. The therapist needs to ask, for example, Who is the abuser and who is the toy today? What triggered these roles and this assignment of roles today? What are the warning signs of danger? Both patient and therapist may avoid playing the helpless or hated party. Inevitably the therapist will become entangled and experience both roles. Allowing the feelings to exist and exploring them gives both parties a chance to rework them. These feelings are sources of deep resonance, which can help the therapist understand the patient's experience, including feelings that may be unpleasant to face. This understanding of the roles being enacted needs to be tentative, at least initially, due to their subjective and unconscious nature.

CHAPTER 14

Is This My Body?
Touch

Humans live and experience life through their body. It is through the early experiences with a person's body that many of their emotional styles are developed (Erikson 1950). People express themselves consciously and unconsciously through their body.

Abused and traumatized patients may ask, "Can I have control over my body? Can it be mine to experience and enjoy for my needs?" This question is related to a previous question, "Can I take control over my own physical and emotional needs?" but is focused on the body. This question is addressed separately because the body is so critical to our experience.

In trauma and abuse, outside forces take over a person's body. Such a person comes to view his or her body as generally controlled by others. Reclaiming ownership is a central goal of treatment.

With traumatic memory, as with developmentally early memory, openings to deeper experience may be keyed to different senses or locations in the body. Recurring patterns of sensation, often experienced in revealing locations in the body, act as precursors of a memory. These patients often seek help for these sensations/affects (or the deep but disconnected/dissociated experience of trauma) from physicians, hospital emergency room staff, and clergy. These memories are embedded in developmental phenomenology and in complex relational contexts and as a result have elaborate meanings and manifestations. This book has described body sensations being explored and finding traumatic memories stored within them (body memories), as illustrated by both Ann's difficulty swallowing and Celeste's vaginal pain, which opened up into memories of profound abuse. The abuse had powerful meanings to these two as developing children about who they were and what was valuable about them.

A physical "dance" occurs in treatment between patient and therapist. This dance is usually overlooked in the supervision and in the literature, but is the source of much useful information. It is evident in where therapists and patients sit, whether they fidget, and how they hold their body and muscles. Flushing and other coloration are helpful indicators of emotional states. This nonverbal communication tends to be less conscious.

TOUCH and Sex

Physical touch is a basic human need. In Erik Erikson's (1950) psychosocial stages, the first stage of trust and mistrust in the world relies on bodily experiences in early childhood. Spitz (1946) found that infants in orphanages who were deprived of touch were highly susceptible to early death. Physical touch can relax, invigorate, and promote physical development. In a physical or sexual abuse patient, this need has been twisted. Touch has been intertwined with violence, coercion, pain, overstimulation, disconnection, and helplessness.

It is at the physical level that abused and traumatized patients experience danger. Many have receded from their bodies into their heads, exhibiting such symptoms as depersonalization and "out-of-body" sensations. Sometimes they hurt themselves because they are not connected to the signals of bodily pain. These patients have distorted thoughts about their bodies—"I am soiled, damaged, repulsive; I am only valuable because my body is a sexual toy."

Abused patients can abandon their bodies and in the process lose the capacity to experience (and empathize with others') ordinary physical sensations.

> In an earlier chapter I discussed a family in which the mother had been abused and was currently mistreating her son. In that illustration, the mother had been regularly beaten as a child to the point where she no longer felt pain when hit. As a result, she could not understand others' fear of being hit or mugged, nor the real impact of her hitting her son. She had also lost the ability to know her own feelings, or find her own words or thoughts, when she was under stress.

> Celeste, who had been massively abused, sometimes burned herself in the bathtub because she had become indifferent to bodily pain and did not fear hot water.

Many abused and traumatized patients cannot enjoy their bodies. This can be related to guilt over sexual feelings, which were characterized as "bad." Sexual feelings may precipitate painful flashbacks, so that sexual feelings are avoided. This may result in loss of orgasmic and other aspects of sexual function as well. Survivors may also live in fear of bodily harm, hiding the body in extensive clothing or gaining excess weight to ward off being assaulted or raped.

These patients may test the therapist's sensibilities about the body. They report experiences that can disgust even the most jaded therapist, such as being forced to eat feces or making unconventional use of bodily fluids. Some patients have written letters to me in their own blood.

DEEPER EXPERIENCE IN THE BODY AND AUXILIARY TREATMENT METHODS

Reich (1945) and Alexander (1950, 1961) emphasized that people develop body functioning and physical styles that incorporate repetitive and traumatic affective experiences. Reich (1945) took this further and stated that all people developed body styles and "body armor" based on emotional experiences, which he believed to be the main ingredients in personality. Reich used these concepts to move the focus of treatment from the mind to the body. Reich conceived of the body as the central point of intervention to change human behavior and functioning. He believed that deep experience can be more effectively opened by body interventions such as breathing and pressure on specific body locations, which then allow the person to access previously unconscious emotional experience and memories. With this emotional access and change in body experience, the person can then be enabled to change emotionally.

This conception of the body's central role in psychological functioning suggests possible treatment techniques that are not usually included within the scope of traditional psychodynamic treatment. The use of other techniques such as breathing, relaxation exercises, meditation, and yoga were emphasized in Celeste's treatment as a way of helping her learn to soothe and reclaim her own body (Perlman 1996b).

> Celeste attended classes in yoga, exercise, and meditation as well as receiving massage therapy from the originally referring body therapist. When she was overwrought she could use these exercises and the sometimes soothing experiences they provided to settle herself down. When Celeste felt intense anxiety, for example, she might take a yoga class or have some sort of body session. Celeste could attend to her emotional self through her bodily self in these ways, and they would often open up new memories and experiences for us to discuss.

The key to the utilization of these auxiliary experiences is always to track and explore the transferential meanings of the patient's behaviors and desires. There are transferences to other figures in the patient's life as well as to other caregivers. These other figures and experiences can be used to run away from treatment or self-regulate the emotional distance from the therapist. This could be motivated by fear of the therapist or a wish to protect the therapist. This auxiliary experience could be a repetition of the traumatic experience (i.e., being molested again) or a reparative experience (i.e., being soothed). This all needs to be explored. One aspect to monitor is that some instructors in these classes may be antipsychotherapy in their rhetoric and as a result place the patient in a dilemma of disobeying one authority or another.

PHYSICAL TOUCH IN TREATMENT

Physical touch in treatment is a very controversial area, one where therapists are open to ethical and legal issues. In response to this, many therapists have become fearful. My hope is that through these currents of social pressure the therapist can keep engaging in treatment in the way that is best for the patient. Some therapists may be comfortable with different levels of contact. Thus, even if physical contact is determined to be in the best interests of the patient, it must also be within the therapist's personal comfort zone. If therapists go beyond their comfort zone, the patient will sense this (which as a result will undermine the therapeutic benefit for the patient). This can then become a mistreatment of the therapist, enacting the abuse with the patient as the perpetrator.

One common issue is how the therapist should respond to the patient who wants to shake hands or hug. This can arise from a patient's need to feel close and loved, or to have a physical experience of the connection. Touch can sometimes be a way of assuming the powers of the therapist. Many fantasies can be embedded in these enactments. These experiences need to be explored for their meaning to the patient, but the timing must be appropriate to the patient's emotional state.

The following example illustrates the patient's need for the soothing function of touch.

> As discussed previously, Celeste felt she needed physical contact, including holding for soothing and containment. I felt that I could not do this, and she found another therapist who would hold her, in conjunction with her work with me. She found the occasional hugs I gave her soothing, and helped contain and integrate the painful affects that were emerging as she relived her traumas.

But touch can also be construed differently by patient and therapist:

> Ann asked for a hug after a difficult session and I gave her one. I felt that I was comforting her. I also felt that I would enjoy it. Later I explored its meaning to her. To my chagrin, she had offered the hug as a present

to ward off my anger over the emotional drain of listening.

Patients need the chance to learn about nontraumatic positive touch. This can be in small part with the therapist. I have usually encouraged patients to have new exploratory experiences in their daily lives. They can begin exploring and touching their own bodies first with their own hands or with objects like towels and cloths, and then move to new touch experiences with their partner or in controlled environments such as massage by another person.

Patients can be physically intimidating. They may encroach on the therapist's space with bear hugs or invade the therapist's privacy. These can be ways of trying to connect more deeply with the therapist in a time of special need, even though the therapist may experience it differently.

Ann found out where I lived and drove by my home, looking through the windows as she passed. It was an unwanted intrusion into my life and my family. She was in a desperate state, so I allowed it to continue until she was out of crisis, at which point I intervened. She needed to feel physically close to me to repeatedly confirm her soothing connection to me.

SELF-MUTILATION AND SUICIDAL BEHAVIOR

Many severely abused and traumatized patients mutilate themselves, or obsess about or attempt suicide; mutilation behavior and suicidal behavior are two distinct phenomena. Either type of behavior can be a reenactment of the trauma, but also may express a variety of internal needs usually related to maintaining self-cohesion.

Mutilation usually involves cutting oneself with a knife or razor blade, or picking or tearing at oneself until bodily damage is done. It can express patients' feelings about themselves, for instance, that they are hateful, that they deserve to be punished, or that some part of them needs to attack another part. The patients may feel they deserve punishment for having submitted, having enjoyed some aspect of the abuse, or having betrayed the abuser by telling. Other times the punishment can be about the therapeutic process. The patients may be punishing themselves for talking to or feeling close to the therapist. Some part, literally and figuratively, of the patient can be telling the patient things such as, "You're a dumb whore for needing and telling your secrets to this man, who will just use you like every other man has. You deserve to be punished for your stupidity."

Mutilating oneself can be an attempt to cope with internal experiences. Some internal states are unbearable: fear of being destroyed or punished by the perpetrator, reexperience of the abuse, humiliation, loss of self-cohesion, a feeling of nonexistence. Mutilation can distract patients from these intolerable states, or terminate them. For example, many patients are overwhelmed by reexperiencing the trauma and lose touch with being alive in the present. The pain of the cuts brings them back to the present almost as the occurrence of the dreaded event releases them from waiting for the repetition of the dreaded event. Other patients do not feel the pain, but the color of their blood can be soothing and preoccupying, and distract them from the reexperience of the trauma. Or this distraction method itself may be the reenacting of how the person survived the trauma. Many of these patients become fragmented and may resort to self-mutilation as their only means to reconstitute.

Patients may mutilate their bodies to enable themselves to function rather than to die. The pain of self-mutilation for these patients may be experienced as emanating from a center of feeling that is deeply rooted in the body and feels genuine, and proves to them that they are alive. In addition, the act of choosing to damage one's own body can help the patient feel control over the experience of the invasion and destruction that is so fearful for many of these patients in their ever-present fear of being retraumatized. In contrast to suicidal behavior, mutilation is usually not life threatening and is therefore handled differently. Therapists may choose not to intervene in self-mutilation. They may wait to explore its underlying meaning and what other behaviors can be substituted before attempting to reduce its frequency.

Therapists need to contain their reactions to self-mutilation so as not to overlook its function in patients' psyche. Yet patients need therapists to be concerned for their welfare as their abusers were not. The therapist may feel helpless to stop this bodily harm, and may be horrified yet fascinated. Usually, the first time therapists deal with this phenomenon they go through "color shock"—a response style on the Rorschach projective test, in which the person is flooded with emotion and unable to function in response to a provocative stimulus. After more experience with severely abused or traumatized patients, therapists come to expect mutilation and ask about it. Generally, I do not treat mutilation as an emergency; however, I am ready to intervene if the behavior risks serious bodily harm to the patient.

Calof (1993) thinks that most patients mutilate themselves during treatment when the therapists have overlooked their anger. Exploring childhood trauma unleashes rage and the desire for revenge, which need an outlet. If none is provided, the rage becomes too overwhelming for patients and is turned against themselves. He recommends setting up rituals in which patients can demolish things (e.g., an old, useless car with hammers or a crowbar) while shouting angrily at the perpetrators.

Suicidal thoughts are usually chronic among these patients. Listening to patients who threaten suicide can frighten therapists. Many therapists overreact, trying to control patients before understanding what the patients are doing. Potential suicide may need to be monitored, but most likely it needs to be understood and accepted as an internal state of distress, rather than an imminent situation that requires intervention. Even when suicide is an imminent threat, I explore its meaning to patients' lives because it is an opening to their core experience. These patients may experience suicidal thoughts as their only source of control. Possibly the patient may feel that the only escape from the pain is death, or that the only way to compel others' attention and acknowledgment, or to get revenge on these others, is self-destruction or suicide. These patients may need this control to combat their feelings of helplessness. This underlying sense of helplessness and disconnection can often be resolved when the patient feels heard.

In general, my experiences with these patients forced me to explore my feelings about personal space, touch, and bodies—my own and other people's. I thought about the difference between caring touch and exploitative touch, and am more aware of how people use their bodies in social interactions. I also realize how differently others may experience touch, and how their reaction may be difficult to predict. Touch and a person's body are complex issues in treatment and should not be ignored.

CHAPTER 15

Can You Believe in Ritual Abuse?*

In confronting the possible existence of ritual abuse of a patient, it is my experience of not knowing whether the reports or other indications of ritual abuse are "real," and having to sit with this uncertainty and confusion for long periods of time, that has been particularly difficult for me. These times of believing and not believing are unnerving, since often it seems that a great deal is riding on the determination of its veracity. This veracity is critical to my assessment of whether the patient is in danger from vicious others, or out of touch with reality. Also, my belief in patients' reports and symptoms may be critical to their ability to hold on to their experience as valid. I don't know whether patients' reports of ritual abuse are warnings to me of real dangers to the patient, and/or to me and my family. Such reports can fill me with such upsetting fantasies that I may feel the need to label them as untrue to stay solidly in the world. This gives rise to so called countertransference issues, which can obstruct my ability to remain open and responsive to what the patient is communicating. These are questions I have never fully put to rest.

The issue of the existence of ritual abuse tests the limits of the therapist's role. Is it a therapist's role to try to determine reality?

Does the therapist have a privileged position in asserting reality to patients? When is it essential for therapists to immerse themselves in the patients' worldview? When is it clinically appropriate for therapists to share with their patients their views of patients' material? When is the therapists' discomfort about their own disbelief important enough to tell the patient that they may disagree with some of the patient's perceptions? Is this an interpretation, a clarification, or just two different subjectivities? How important is timing in this process? When are patients interested in the therapist's beliefs?

Ritual abuse is defined here as the sexual abuse, torture, and exploitation of children for the purpose of a secret cult-like group. The abuse can be of a horrendous nature (e.g., cannibalism of babies) and can include large, organized conspiracies designed to hide these activities.

The issue of whether ritual abuse exists is controversial. Some authorities see stories of ritual abuse as fantasies. Some investigative newspaper articles and other publications (e.g., Wright 1993) have found no evidence to support these allegations. They conceive of ritual-abuse stories as the invention of frightened and suggestible people who express their deep fears through metaphors, and mobilize others to participate in their hysteria.

Others view ritual abuse as a real and even common occurrence; they feel that the professional community denies its existence and is too easily dissuaded by propaganda devised to cover it up. These believers have developed textbooks, evidence, and treatment methodologies for ritual abuse (e.g., Young et al. 1991).

Coming to some solid and comfortable position within this controversy has been elusive for me. In my taking the reader into this realm, I feel uncertain and that I am constantly on thin ice.

I was somewhat skeptical about the existence of ritual abuse when I began my first ritual abuse treatment experience. Through these experiences, however, I have become more of a believer. Some of the time I think that ritual abuse is hard to believe, not because there is no evidence of it, but because the feelings it brings up are difficult to tolerate. In this frame of mind I point to historical precedents. Although it is comforting to blame Hitler for the Holocaust, many people were involved in the killing, which was rationalized as the semireligious pretext of cleansing the Aryan race. Many in the world ignored or denied this information.

More recently, the newspapers were filled with stories of the Waco disaster in Texas, which involved a cult that sexually abused children to fulfill religious beliefs. This cult remained secret for many years until it was literally blown up in public. In my women's groups in the heroin treatment center, common stories involved parents prostituting their children for money or drugs. In this frame of mind, I can easily ask myself why not believe that children are tortured and misused for the large sums of money that child prostitution and pornography generate, under the cover of some religious pretext and rituals? These profitable organizations vary in their sophistication and size. They may take extensive measures to protect themselves, including hypnosis, brainwashing, and discrediting the testimony of victims. With this perspective, I am upset to feel that so many powerful people are decisively denying such atrocities and that the victims are not getting help.

I feel very ambivalent. How far I can go with these ideas depends on my experience from moment to moment. I find myself trying not to think about these issues. Both believing and not believing feels upsetting.

When working with patients who claim to be victims of ritual abuse, I sometimes experience them as telling me their fears, hopes, and needs through concretized images of their inner dramas. At these moments I feel that part of the torture they are suffering now is a conflict between their own dissociated self states, which haunt them. These dissociated states may have been born of trauma and abuse, but perhaps not the ritual abuse that these patients describe. Other moments I believe that the torture that adults perpetrated on these patients is being acted out in the transference, with the details of the ritual abuse being in part a metaphoric, but emotionally accurate, reenactment.

At these moments I wonder whether I am so ungrounded as to be so easily carried away by my patients' beliefs, losing my own reality and collapsing into theirs. At times I have been fully convinced of one perspective and then have lost conviction in that perspective and become persuaded by another; my perspective can depend, it seems, on the views of the person with whom I am talking. Maintaining the approval of the other person influences my belief systems for that interaction. From this vantage point, I am concerned for my patients who are out of touch and living a "daily torture." I am concerned that my susceptibility to the others (e.g., patients) risks confirming their perspectives and nightmares, and in this way I am failing to help them escape from and see alternatives to their subjective horrors. In short, I sometimes fear that my permeability and motivation to adapt to others may result in my colluding with my patients' nightmares.

Many times patients' willingness to discuss their beliefs depends on their sense of whether therapists are open to listening and entertaining the ideas they present. From patients' perspective they need to develop trust. They must navigate openings with the therapist before they feel safe enough to discuss their belief, for example, that they were ritually abused. Usually patients feel that telling the therapist about ritual abuse is a risk. Many fear that therapists will think that they are crazy or will reject them. Patients may feel that to report ritual abuse is a threat to their well-being, that the perpetrators may kill them (or the loved therapist) to keep their secrets. To tell their stories, these patients need confidence that therapists will manage the situation in a way that protects them both.

In my experience, ritual-abuse material engenders the most countertransference. It also takes a toll on the therapist. Here is a vignette from the treatment of my first ritual-abuse patient.

As described earlier, Celeste started treatment with her prior therapist because she had chronic vaginal and other bodily pains. Over time, she experienced emerging memories of sexual abuse by her father. Her therapist responded that Celeste was too suggestible to the newspapers she read. Unhappy with this response and other aspects of treatment, she came to see me. I treated her for more than three years, five to seven times per week.

The first year of Celeste's treatment focused on her abuse by her father. Then a new personality, Mary, emerged, speaking and behaving like a 4-year-old. Mary began to draw pictures and write about her experiences. Mary described the following in Celeste's diary with another personality's help:

"[A little girl] enduring torturous horror of the night. Mommy spanked me on my bare fanny—fanny is a polite word. It's okay to say it, but not butt. I had a butt and a cunt. I hate that word, and my butt aches very badly. I like the safety of my wall next to my bed. I slept pressed up against it; it felt safe and firm and like it wouldn't move . . . . Terror of someone coming into the bathroom. My whole body feels scared and I can't breathe . . . . The victim was a rectum where things were stuck up and the pain and the pleasure were intense. My mommy was never there to hear my silent nightly screams."

I was still surprised by the emergence of new personalities and what the personalities told me about her father's and now her mother's behavior. (This parental behavior was in the past but to some personalities the past was the present.) The following dream captured Celeste's fear of the multiple personalities and other dissociative material that was emerging: "Art all over, lines, colors, craziness. A little girl draws others attached to her, and then she says, any therapy without the knowledge of these others is dangerous. Other parts of this girl—me. The other parts want to come out, but there is fear of not being able to hold the self together."

The first drawing (Figure 15–1) was of her mother's face. Her mother's face fills the entire page, and shows large teeth and extreme agitation. The patient stated that her mother was angry at Mary for drawing, and that she "hit and hit" Mary. What we determined later was that as a little girl Mary was drawing pictures of the abuse that was happening to her, and that her mother punished her for doing so.

Then Mary drew Figure 15–2 of her mother, in a black robe with large agitated teeth, putting a cross up Mary's "hole" (vagina). I was shocked by these emerging memories of ritual abuse. I was having trouble believing that this could all be true. Sessions had to be increased to seven days a week because she kept calling me on days when she had no session. I felt unable to cleanse myself of her images. I had difficulty orienting to my daily life and family, and even at times to other patients.

Figure 15–1

Here is a dream I had in reaction to this treatment: A crazy patient of mine has stolen everything out of our house. I am in great distress. He took cars, a coin collection, and got into my office and vandalized it. I need to see my analyst, but what can he do?

Hearing about the ritual abuse made me feel out of control, and at times I felt more comfortable thinking that the patient was psychotic. Her treatment threatened to take away my sense of inner peace and equilibrium. It reminded me of seeing my siblings beaten, and fearing that they would be murdered before my eyes.

Celeste's other personalities came out and drew Figure 15–3. The writing on the picture says "Training with blood scary terror." Blood issues from the arm of the hooded person and the kneeling child. These people were cutting off others' arms to use the blood in rituals of sex and violence with children. This picture, along with Figure 15–5, below, and the report of some of the personalities, evidences the cult nature of the rituals.

Figure 15-2

Figure 15–4 also was drawn later. It illustrates part of the technique I used with this patient. She would not draw unless I drew. My drawing was a concrete demonstration that I was not her mother, and would not punish her for drawing (Celeste depicted such punishment in Figure 15–1). In Figure 15–4, I drew myself at the beach on a sunny day, watching sailboarders. At that time I did not realize I was depicting my fantasy of where I wanted to escape, namely away from her material.

Figure 15–5 is a close-up of the material I was avoiding. The words in the picture are "_____'s house was scary" (name blocked out for confidentiality). An alter of Celeste's described being escorted from school to this person's home, where there were crosses and people torturing children. The children were threatened with terrible things if they informed others about these activities.

Figure 15-4

Figure 15-5

Celeste discussed sexual and other punishments the cult followers used when she disobeyed, including tearing her body and threatening to kill her, her loved ones, or her pets. She would relive some of these moments with heart-wrenching affects and intense body experiences. Listening to some descriptions, like killing babies and having to eat parts of them, or being buried alive, disturbed me more than other descriptions. This image conjured thoughts of the friend who died in the bus crash after I switched seats with him. I dreamed I was buried alive in his casket with the maggots that had eaten his body, and woke up screaming. This material emerged while I was seeing Celeste seven days a week during an almost two-year period.

Together we called the child-abuse hotline and filed a report, although it increased both our fears. We felt it was important for the sake of future victims. At this moment in treatment I believed her story literally.

Celeste displayed many personalities, male and female, from 2-year-olds to adults. At least one male personality wanted to kill her for reporting the cult and its abuse. He saw death as preferable to the tortures that the cult might inflict if they found out that the patient had betrayed them. The patient's distress over this material devastated her relationship with her father, mother, and siblings. She also had difficulty functioning as a wife or mother.

Over time, different personalities worked together to fit the pieces into a whole picture. Some extracts from her diary tell the story:

"My father sexually abused me . . . . [I was] used in child prostitution and child pornography from age 3 on. I have memories of daily sexual abuse and endless torture that my father felt was done to strengthen me. As an infant to 6 years old, my mother took me every Sunday to this church. I was ritually abused at that church by the women in the nursery. One of the ministers would take me from the class and tell me I was one of God's chosen and then he would proceed to rape me at the church . . . . [I remember] being burned with candles, crosses being jammed up me vaginally, being burned and having pins inserted into every area of my body, having animals and babies killed in front of me and being forced to eat their raw flesh and drink their blood. . . . My mother was given instructions on forms of punishment to give me at home if I did not do what was prescribed.

"As I got older I was used as a front for laundering illegal cult money (drugs, porno, baby selling, etc.) and I feel I was used to move money around from bank to bank."

My reactions to the presentation and processing of this material fluctuated. At times, the stories of programming, ritual abuse, and training to become a "high priestess" sounded crazy. I felt relief as I attributed these ideas to her being out of touch.

I was bolstered by newspaper articles stating that investigations of specific allegations of ritual abuse uncovered no supporting evidence (e.g., "County Panel Scrutinized for Satanic Claims," Los Angeles Times, December 13, 1992, p. B-1). Many professionals have concluded that these patients must be delusional. Putnam (1991), a respected authority on child abuse treatment and dissociative disorders, concluded that there is insufficient evidence to verify the existence of large, organized groups of ritual abusers. Further, he states that part of the phenomenon can be attributed to contagious panic.

I wavered when I was confronted with such information. Yet the explanations offered by my ritual-abuse patients (I have seen two) made sense, and I began to believe their stories. I read more widely, trying to make sense of my experience. Some thoughts and points in the literature are highlighted. In many cases, corroborating information has increased the validity of these types of claims. For example, other patients have reported the same patterns of ritual abuse, such as live burial as part of the training. The material I encountered was consistent with the findings of other clinicians who have treated ritual-abuse victims. For example, Young and colleagues (1991) concluded that these patterns are consistent and true. In many cases, family members have confirmed aspects of what happened. One criterion I use to help decide the psychic veracity of the material reported is to observe whether exploring the material reduces symptoms and promotes a sense of deeper self-cohesion. This occurred when I explored this material with Celeste.

Sometimes I felt as if I were drowning in a cesspool. I found that when I had sessions with Celeste seven days a week I could not free myself of the images she graphically described, and I would become depressed. I needed one day a week without contact with Celeste and her frightening (surreal) world in order to continue the work.

I had another dream in reaction to what Celeste reported: All these doctors are captured by Nazis in World War II, and many cooperate and become just like Nazis, with red buttons and eating human flesh, especially arms. The Americans conquer the Nazis and the captain who enters the camp threatens trials and finds lots of evidence.

Celeste's material stimulated my fear of others and my hope that evil people would be caught and convicted.

My wife became resentful for the first time in my clinical career and in our relationship. She asked me to reduce the weekend sessions. I felt I could not reduce sessions, because I feared that Celeste might kill herself. Eventually, feeling that she was at imminent risk for suicide, I had Celeste hospitalized. This was the first time in years that I had hospitalized a patient. I felt relieved and slept soundly. Her insurance was very limited, however, and we quickly used up her lifetime cap on psychiatric hospitalization. Also, her children needed her. So we proceeded on an outpatient basis, and the same exhausting and overwhelming process occurred again. I gradually became depleted again. I was not in formal treatment at the time, but had begun consulting with a colleague twice a week, helping each other with issues, personal and professional. He told me to refer Celeste to another therapist for my own well-being. I felt I could not do so, but everywhere I turned I got the same advice.

Celeste feared that the material might overwhelm me and that the cult might hurt me. She related the following dream: "I feel so little and so panicked; such bad things happened and I'm afraid that Stuart will leave me. I'm too disgusting and this could hurt him and I love Stuart and don't want anything bad to happen to him."

In the following diary entry, Celeste expressed her feelings about the several therapists she had seen before me: "Ninety-nine percent of therapists are blown out of the water by this material."

Celeste believed that there was a well-organized group willing to mutilate, torture, and kill for its own gain and survival. If I believed her story I would often experience intense countertransference reactions, including fear that my family or I would be killed or, worse, buried alive.

As Celeste progressed through the treatment, I felt proud of her emerging strength and her ability to wrest control of herself from this malevolent organization. This was confirmed in her following dream: "I am going to a healer and he is healing me." She points to her vaginal area. "He says, 'I'll give you the right ovary—not that you need to know.' "

At other times when I was skeptical, Celeste threatened that if I could not come along on her journey, she would find a therapist who could. I felt I had to comply and believe or else, as if I would be disobeying my mother.

Celeste opened my eyes to experiences that I had never imagined. Through the evocative power of empathy and transference, I experienced parts of what she described. I needed the help of others to survive this journey, and had not imagined that conducting treatment could be so stressful. I have become more aware of my own vulnerabilities.

I was seeing both Celeste and Ann during a three-year period, and both were in constant crisis. Late in this treatment period, I received a powerful piece of information. I had been treating Z, who had fantasies of having sex with children, but denied having acted on them. I believed

Z. Z stopped coming to treatment. I was informed that Z had been convicted of abusing children during the time I had been seeing Z. I used
this information as an indictment of my clinical skills. I felt responsible
for the "destruction" of others, as in the bus accident. I fell into self-recrimination and guilt. My clinical work began to feel too much to handle.

For the first time, I lost my empathy. I could not listen to my patients
and thought I might have to give up being a therapist. I became depressed and as a result lost a few patients. I also stopped taking new
patients for a time. It took me several months and my own treatment to
regain my empathy. I was resistant to hearing Ann's and Celeste's
material because these images were entering me, creating nightmares
and insomnia. I unconsciously made some empathic blunders that tem-
porarily pushed both Ann and Celeste away. When I became more centered, both treatments resumed. I reduced Celeste's treatment to five
days per week and Ann's to four. This arrangement was more tolerable;
I became my old self again. I have retained a residual awareness of my
own limits.

Many years later, I am still in touch with Celeste. She feels integrated
and happy working with survivor groups, and training professionals on
working with ritual-abuse survivors. She periodically shares her ideas
about effective treatment with me.

Some patients and therapists who believe in ritual abuse see danger and the cult everywhere. Any person who does not believe is seen
as "cult-influenced." This belief can become contagious. The task is to
contain it and not be overwhelmed.

To accept ritual abuse and its implications is to glimpse a darker side
of life. Accepting it has changed me. Often, I would like to deny its existence, and sometimes do, with relief.

PART III

EMOTIONAL SURVIVAL

Some treatment experiences can be emotionally threatening to the therapist's well-being. Surviving these experiences in such a way that enables the therapist to be a positive force for the patient is critical to long-term treatment. Some over-extension can be tolerated for periods, but prolonged stress and strain on the therapist without appropriate support and coping strategies can destroy the treatment for the patient and result in burnout for the therapist. In these last two chapters, some practical strategies for maintaining the therapist's well being emotionally, physically, financially, and legally are proposed.

Chapter 16, "Reality, Countertransference, and the False Memory Controversy: Guidelines," presents a clinical perspective on the controversy, reviews the relevant literature on memory, and elucidates practical clinical guidelines. Given all the lawsuits and dissension in this area of treatment, the therapist needs to have some grounding in how to manage these issues, for they have powerful implications for treatment and the therapist's own personal well-being.

Chapter 17, "Therapist Survival: Concluding Perspectives and Strategies," offers some general conclusions and guidelines for the therapist's emotional survival. Included in this chapter are some approaches of my own that I have used to avoid burnout in this very difficult field. These strategies may or may not fit the needs of other therapists.

CHAPTER 16

Reality, Countertransference, and the False Memory Controversy: Guidelines*

*This chapter is adapted from "'Reality' and Countertransference in the Treatment of Sexual Abuse Patients: The False Memory Controversy" by S. D. Perlman, in the *Journal of the American Academy of Psychoanalysis* 24(1): 115–135, copyright © 1996 by the American Academy of Psychoanalysis and used by permission.

Controversies concerning repressed, delayed, or false memories of sexual abuse in childhood have dominated newspaper headlines and TV talk shows recently. Lawsuits against parents by adult children, or against priests or teachers, are becoming more common. Parents who say they have been falsely accused of child abuse are suing the therapists of their accusing children. Patients are accusing their therapists of planting memories. Other patients are suing previous therapists for not uncovering repressed memories. There are many organizations of survivors for mutual support. Now there is even an organization called the False Memory Syndrome (FMS) Foundation, which helps persons to sue therapists involved in uncovering memories that the organization believes are false memories. How can we make sense of all of this? How do therapists continue their work within this crossfire?

All of the uproar can have an adverse effect on the therapeutic process, impacting both the patient and the therapist. Therapists who treat patients who have suffered abuse are at considerable risk of lawsuit. For example, in June 1994, in a Napa Valley, California, court decision called the Ramona Case, the therapist of a patient who had memories of incest was found guilty of malpractice. The grounds for the malpractice judgment were that the therapist had allegedly used leading techniques with the patient, and that the therapist had allegedly established conflicting treatment relationships in the manner in which the confrontation session with the reported perpetrator had been implemented. The plaintiff, the accused father, received $500,000. During that time period, many therapists were less able to believe the stories of abuse that their own patients told them. For example, Ann came into therapy feeling distraught and worried that no one would believe her reports of abuse; she even feared that I might turn against her as her previous therapist had. She may have sensed my fear as well as her own. I imagined being sued and having to pay a large settlement out of personal funds, and was shaken. (For an in-depth description of the cycles of belief and denial in the patient and analyst in the treatment of sexual abuse and multiple personality disorder, see Perlman 1993, 1995.)

The following are two examples of a growing false memory literature. A False Memory Syndrome Foundation brochure has the following definition of false memory syndrome:

> FMS is a condition in which a person's identity and relationships are centered around the memory of a traumatic experience which is objectively false but the person strongly believes it to be true. It has a devastating effect on the victim and typically produces a continuing dependency on the therapeutic program that created the syndrome.

It is a terrible thing for a therapist to feel that he or she might be hurting a patient or planting false beliefs. There is even an implication in the above quote that the therapist implants these false memories for financial gain.

A *New Yorker* article by Lawrence Wright entitled "Remembering Satan" (May 17 and 24, 1993) details what the author called a current-day Salem witch hunt. Wright describes how two teenage girls accused their father and several members of the police force of sexual and satanic ritual abuse. There were several court cases and many investigations. Little evidence of an objective nature was found, especially of the satanic ritual abuse. According to Wright, even though no real court evidence beyond the two girls' testimony was found, the father was convicted and the family destroyed. The article portrays these teenagers as suggestible, confused, and swayed by overzealous police and church members. Yet on appeal, after these articles were published, the court upheld the father's conviction. This makes it hard to know what to believe.

In this area the literature is so polarized there is almost no middle ground. This chapter is a response to this literature, which I believe is in danger of trying to rectify some problems in this treatment area by "throwing the baby out with the bath water." The baby here is the real patient. It is important to understand the source of the memory controversy, so as to better deal with countertransference issues and the construction of reality that takes place in the treatment of sexual abuse victims in a way that reduces the likelihood of excesses without retraumatizing them or misdiagnosing other patients as sexual abuse victims. I present a communications model from which to examine the memory controversy, and then review research and literature on each of the communications model's stages. Given the difficulty in making judgments about the believability of the clinical material in this area, criteria for making this judgment are proposed. From these sources, I draw some conclusions and recommend guidelines for coping with the many problems and paradoxes related to this complex issue.

COMMUNICATIONS MODEL

The memory controversy may be more fruitfully looked at from a communications model. That is, how can we best understand the difficulties of communicating pain and hurt from one person to another? I would like to look at each of the stages of this process in such a way as to help clarify common patterns in childhood sexual abuse.

The first stage in the process is the event itself. What were the characteristics of the actual traumatic event? Specifically, what are the special circumstances of the sexually abused child and the typical family and social patterns associated with this type of abuse that severely affect the ability of the victim to remember, believe, and speak about the abuse?

The second stage in this process is memory. To communicate in the present about an event that happened in the past, the event must be encoded into memory. How memory works may be different than is commonly thought; recent research in this area may shed new light on the memory controversy, clarifying some of the confusion.

The third stage in this process is the victim's decision to speak. If patients remember abuse, they must decide to tell the therapist or analyst. The willingness of patients to speak, and the ability of the analyst to hear, is affected by a variety of factors in sexual abuse. These patients have a life history of having been betrayed in the most fundamental of human relationships over and over again, and therefore they do not trust others; they are reluctant to self-disclose.

Speaking is the next stage in the communications model. Actually forming the words and presenting them in an interpersonal context of therapy can be a very difficult experience. The intense content and trauma in sexual abuse may make patients and analysts not wish to experience the feelings brought up by the material, and avoid or interrupt the process of telling.

The fifth and final stage in the process is believing and holding the material once it is spoken. Two factors in sexual abuse push for suppression of the abuse material. One factor is the serious implications for many aspects of the life of the patient—personal, familial, financial, and legal. The implications for the analyst in terms of lawsuits and other factors is also powerful. Finally, believing and disbelieving the reported material is a cyclic and difficult process. In this chapter I give general criteria for helping to make this important clinical decision.

THE EVENT AND THE SPECIAL CIRCUMSTANCES OF SEXUAL ABUSE

The first stage in the communications model is the occurrence of the event and how its characteristics affect the patient's ability to remember, believe, and speak. Usually, the sexual abuse of children is perpetrated by someone the victim knows and even loves: parents or stepparents, friends, neighbors, or other family members. In situations of chronic abuse, the child not only has to endure the abuse but has to behave as if nothing is happening, for example, during the day or in the presence of others. This charade may be enforced by threats and punishment. The split between the denial of the day and the fear and abuse of the night is internalized, making the abuse material difficult to access by the more normal-appearing self.

The person coming into therapy may not have any access to the worst traumas that occurred. It may be necessary to engage dissociated self states in which the traumatic memories are separated off from the person's awareness. The sexual abuse constitutes an invasion of boundaries, confusing the person's ability to maintain a separate identity, which induces self-doubting. This is compounded if the person is told he or she is crazy. A *Los Angeles Times* (1985) survey documented that the vast majority of victims who told an adult about the abuse were told that they were lying and/or crazy, and were not offered help. In a slightly different study, this basic negative response was confirmed. Hanks et al. (1988), in a study of children who had been abused and had come to the attention of the authorities, found that many parents' and adults' initial response to the child's disclosure was one of disbelief, often of a punitive nature. "Adults interpret the children's descriptions often as either lies or fantasies, and respond with remarks like: 'of course Daddy does not hurt your bottom with a knife' when a 2-year-old girl had told her mother and social worker that 'my Daddy cut my tuppence with a knife' " (Hanks et al. 1988, p. 148).

These victims may fear the loss of their families. They may also see themselves as bad, as the cause of all bad things and deserving of punishment. They may be left with doubts and/or negative convictions about their abilities; they cannot believe themselves. They come to treatment with the expectation that the therapist will not believe them. The transference often becomes a reenactment of aspects of the abusive relationships that the patient experienced in childhood.

MEMORY PROCESS AND ENCODING TRAUMA

The second stage in the communications model is the memory process. There are several different areas of research literature that can help us understand the memory process more fully.

Declarative and Procedural Memory

Psychoanalytic researchers, including Beebe (1993) and Emde and colleagues (1991), have synthesized research findings that point to two parallel types of memory. Clyman (1992), an associate of Emde, wrote an extensive review article of these two memory systems, drawing on neurological evidence. One system is verbally articulated and integrated, and is referred to as "declarative memory." It starts to function around the age of 3 or 4, and is based on the maturation of part of the brain called the hippocampus. The second memory system, called "procedural memory," contains kinesthetically encoded bodily experiences, and is present from birth. This concept of a dual memory system has implications about what memories are available and how they can be accessed, based on the type of experience and the age of the person at the time of the experience. One implication is that early experiences are more likely to be encoded bodily and somatically in comparison to later experiences, which have higher levels of verbal content. This also implies that prior to 3 years of age, almost all memories are stored in a procedural, unconscious, bodily oriented memory system.

The neurobiological studies from which these concepts of procedural and declarative memory-type systems were derived are primarily associated with Squire and his associates (Squire 1986, 1987).

Traumatic Memory

A second line of research and clinical literature on combat trauma converges with this first group on types of memory. The connection between trauma and body experiences was reasserted after World War II with research centered on the treatment of posttraumatic stress disorder (Herman 1992). The concept of repression did not seem to work well when assessing the effects of combat trauma (Cohen 1985). These patients had dream images and body experiences that seemed to be flashbacks of unsymbolized traumatic occurrences. Following this line of thinking, Davies (1994) and Davies and Frawley (1994) attempted to synthesize and refocus the psychoanalytic literature, bringing together work on sexual abuse trauma, brain function, and dissociation. Davies and Frawley explain that traumatic memories are not processed and are usually stored without being integrated into overall memory, in an unelaborated, nonsymbolic sensory form. When the memory is processed with the analyst, it becomes available to being turned into what we usually think of as a memory. This process could be called "creating a memory" with the patient, from the stored sensory fragments (P. Giovacchini, personal communication, 1994). Davies and Frawley's summary of the biological brain research on memory also indicates that there may be more than two separate systems of memory: a verbal logical memory in the hippocampal system, and a traumatic unintegrated memory, as well as a memory system like the procedural memory system highlighted by Clyman (1992).

This is consistent with what I have observed in my own clinical work. In previous articles, I have highlighted the somatization process in sexual abuse victims, and the difficulty that victims have expressing these unprocessed traumatic memories. This can be seen in the material from Ann's analysis, presented in previous chapters. I have also addressed the issue of the analyst's belief or disbelief of patients' accounts of traumatic abuse, and how this affects the opening up of these traumatic states, as well as the forms the somatic expression take (Perlman 1993, 1995, 1996a).

Dissociation

Dissociation is noteworthy because, as indicated earlier, the memories of trauma may be encapsulated in a separate dissociated self state, and therefore are not repressed memories but instead are dissociated memories. When the dissociated self state is present, memories of the trauma will be present. When that self state leaves, the memories of the trauma may also leave consciousness completely. This may only change when the self state containing the traumatic material is integrated with the other aspects of the personality.

Memory Research Specific to Sexual Abuse

There has been other work on the memory process that focuses specifically on sexual abuse memories. This is a very controversial literature that has been reviewed by a number of different researchers who have come to exactly opposite conclusions.

One set of studies done by Williams (1992) documents that severe abuse can be forgotten. She conducted a research project using hospital records. She followed up on child abuse victims who had been brought to a hospital emergency room six to ten years earlier for emergency medical treatment. She found that one-third of the patients did not remember the abuse or being brought to the emergency room. Some victims remembered exact details of what happened to them, but sincerely believed that the abuse had occurred to another person they knew, such as a cousin.

Herman and Schatzow (1987) conducted a study of 54 incest survivors, of whom approximately 75 percent were able to find outside corroborating evidence of their abuse. Terr's studies of documented trauma, summarized in 1994, suggested that there was a generally accurate recollection of the trauma, but there were some problems of distortion of isolated details among some children. She documented this in the Chowchilla kidnapping case. In this case, all of the children remembered being kidnapped, but some children mistakenly remembered the wrong number of kidnappers, or had inaccurate memories of the details of the physical scene on follow-up, some time later.

Spanos and Borgess (1994) and Loftus (1992) challenged this research with their own research. These studies revealed the suggestibility of subjects to having details of presented and recalled material changed. Terr (1994) critiqued Spanos and Borgess's and Loftus's research. She doubted whether these laboratory studies with college volunteers are actually relevant to traumatic situations experienced in real life. Terr pointed out that what Loftus and Spanos and Borgess demonstrated in their studies is consistent with Terr's own research findings. Loftus and Spanos and Borgess demonstrated that when pressured, adults and children will distort details of material that is presented. Terr concluded that Loftus and Spanos and Borgess did not demonstrate that the person forgets or distorts the overall experience.

Faller (1992) and Perry (1992) each reviewed the research on child and youth abuse memories and interviewing strategies involved in child abuse reporting. Using detailed research findings, both demonstrated that with direct questioning a child's memory looks inferior to an adult's memory, but when structured questions are used, asking the child about time, place, and order, the child's memories are as good as adult recall (e.g., Saywitz 1992).

This research seems to indicate that the basic memory process in adults, and to a lesser degree in children, can and should be considered generally accurate, but subject to distortion under pressure. The next stage of the communications model is the decision to speak.

THE DECISION TO SPEAK: BETRAYAL AND THE NEED FOR SECRECY

Survivors of child sexual abuse have experienced real human traumas. These patients often believe that people are highly capable of abusive behavior and that the best strategy for survival is to assume that bad things will happen, so as not to be caught unaware. Therefore, vigilant self-protection is seen as a survival necessity. Their central organizing principle is often that the therapist and others are untrustworthy and will hurt them. With this expectation, it is difficult for abuse victims to share their most painful abuse experiences with the therapist. Consciously or unconsciously, many patients feel extremely vulnerable, and use secrecy and a false persona as the safest and smartest strategy for self-protection. It is only after the patient has extensively tested the trustworthiness of the analyst that the traumatic memories emerge. My experience is that it may take years to find out the whole story. The patient may feel intense shame, humiliation, and a deep sense that it was his or her innate badness that caused the abuse. This fits with a child's egocentric view of self and the world, and it also fits with what abusers often tell their child victims.

SPEAKING: FEAR AND OVERSTIMULATION

As reported earlier, the *Los Angeles Times* study showed how the attempts of the child to tell others about the abuse resulted in attacks on the child and no constructive help. This then is the common expectation of the patient as the abuse is described to the therapist or analyst. The childhood retraumatization for telling, I believe, is reenacted with the therapist by retractions and then reassertions of the memories of abuse.

Analysts often become confused about their patients' sexual abuse memories, because of the patients' fears and uncertainties. Many patients enter therapy with no memories of abuse, with only vague feelings of anxiety. As the memories of the abuse emerge, the patient may experience pain, cycles of belief and denial, frenzy, uncertainty, and fearfulness. These feelings can be hard to contain for everyone involved.

It is difficult to listen to horrible instances of abuse related by incest victims. Hearing stories about how the abuser raped, tied up the helpless child, and exploited him or her can provoke much latent unresolved conflict in the analyst, as discussed in this book. These upsetting reactions need to be managed during a therapy session.

BELIEVING AND HOLDING OF THE MATERIAL: IMPLICATIONS OF THE ABUSE FOR THE PATIENT AND ANALYST

The final stage of the communication model is the believing and holding of the material. Opening up memories of abuse is a disorienting experience for a patient. It can unravel the story of the patient's life, disrupt relationship patterns, and compromise the existing construction of his or her own self. Similarly, the analyst's view of the patient can be unhinged if the abuse was not suspected. Even the analyst's own worldview can be disrupted on hearing of extreme traumas.

The patient experiences many fears as a result of abuse: loss of identity, loss of the fantasy of a good childhood, loss of connection to parents, public shame and humiliation, and possible physical attack from perpetrators. A common pattern is that the patient is too fearful to explore the abuse memories until the perpetrator has died or become incapacitated. The patient may fear that the abuser might retaliate for the disclosure of the crimes. This fear can be overcome if the therapist appears to the patient to be a strong and supportive ally. The therapist becomes the most important and at times the only close relationship in the patient's life.

It is not always clear how to decide what is reality and what is fantasy, and what the appropriate response in the clinical situation should be. Many therapists agonize, feeling caught in a trap of not knowing what is clinically indicated, fearing that they may hurt the patient or the patient's family while trying to help.

In the area of sexual abuse, determining whether something that the patient says is true has tremendous implications, not just for the patient's life but for the therapist's as well. For example, if patients tell the therapist that they were sexually abused by their parents, and the parents run a day-care center, this raises moral issues for the analyst, as well as legal implications. The analyst may have to file a child abuse report, an act that deeply impacts the relationship the analyst has with the patient. This can be a very validating experience for the patient. The patient may experience the report as evidence the therapist believes the patient and will act on the patient's behalf. This child abuse report will also affect the patient's parents, their day-care center, and possibly all of the families who have their children at the center. If, as typically happens, the parents who are accused deny the accusations, a major struggle and possible police action will result; legal battles may ensue, and the analyst may be sued, or may have to testify in court or write reports that become public record. The judgment and professionalism of the therapist may become the center of this legal battle, and there may be malpractice suits from any number of possible sources on any number of grounds. This may result in stressful situations for the therapist, such as depositions, legal costs, or even financial loss or public sanction and humiliation. There may be implications in these situations that the therapist is too open to being "taken over" by the patient's beliefs. Fear of this is sufficient to create strong countertransference.

At times, for very specific clinical interventions, the clinician must assess whether the material presented is probably true or false. Guidelines for this are proposed below.

WHEN ARE MEMORIES LESS LIKELY
TO BE REALITY BASED?

It is important to move the debate over the accuracy of memories from determining whether distortions occur, to acknowledging distortions and determining when they are most likely to occur, and determining how distortions can be distinguished from more accurate abuse memories.

The therapist has a pressing practical need to determine which factors affect the likelihood of the distortion of memories. This is because therapists are working in a difficult legal climate, and must adhere to reporting requirements in most states. Many states require therapists to report suspected abuse within hours, even if the therapist is unsure of the veracity of the memories. The penalties for noncompliance are severe.

In attempting to discriminate between distortions and accurate abuse memories, care should be taken not to retraumatize patients who have had the courage to overcome their fears and risk standing up in the world to say that they were abused, facing their own fear and the wrath of the perpetrator. In my experience and that of my colleagues, there are few false reports. I am defining false memory as the situation when the patient recants the memories and maintains this for years, believing that they were not true after all.

Although I have seen many patients with memories of sexual

abuse, I personally have had only two persons report that they had false memories. One came to believe this under the threat of legal action; after the threat was gone, the patient returned to belief in the memories. A second patient had great difficulty over the years accepting her own images and feelings of abuse. She decided over time that she had been abused. She then was uncertain as to who the abuser or abusers were. Over the course of therapy she had periods when she was certain that the abuser had been her father; however, at other periods she became convinced that she had instead been abused by her brothers. It is important that the therapist realize that it is a possibility that the patient's certainty about the identity of the abuser can shift over time. My experience is that, especially when the abuser has threatened the victim to keep him or her from telling about the abuse, there can such be intense fear that the victim experiences an almost "hysterical blindness" in relation to the face of the abuser. In addition, in my experience, the patients who have been sexually abused by both parents usually remember only the father's abuse, and only later remember the more upsetting ideas that their mother participated as well.

A common theme in the literature regarding assessing whether sexual abuse has occurred is that sexual abuse in childhood tends to produce a full syndrome of long-lasting symptoms. This syndrome presents as a complete package. Therefore, if a clinician sees a patient exhibiting one symptom without the rest of the syndrome, in my opinion, this goes against the diagnosis of sexual abuse. This differential diagnosis has been written about for the last 100 years; some of this literature is described below.

Far from being a new phenomenon, the false memory controversy has plagued psychoanalysis since Freud's first psychoanalytic paper, "The Aetiology of Hysteria" (1896). In this paper and others, Freud espoused the seduction theory (1887–1902, 1896a–c), in which he stated that the shock of intense sexual stimulation in childhood, often the result of incest or molestation by family members, specifically causes hysteria. (This is discussed in Chapter 1.) In this work Freud constantly refers to colleagues and others who might accuse him of planting the ideas of sexual assault in his patients' minds. He

Freud, as well as more recent writers, such as Meiselman (1978), have described common family and intergenerational patterns in sexual abuse. A few traits mentioned are secrecy, isolation threats, parental jealousy, and alcohol use.

In this section I will survey some of the signs that indicate that abuse memories may be false. Individuals may have something to gain by making false claims, for example, or patients may be responding to their therapists' unconscious needs. Individuals with a clear vested interest will sometimes use a charge of sexual abuse for gain. For example, I am told by child abuse workers and court custody evaluators that divorce and custody battles are especially fertile ground for one party to try to discredit the other through the use of false child abuse accusations. However, the child's behavior and testimony in these cases usually does not fit the overall profile associated with abuse. Also the child's testimony will probably lack affective intensity.

The patient who is most vulnerable to inadvertent false memory input is one who has doubts about his or her perceptions of reality, and has great dependency needs. This is a patient who feels that his or her life depends on getting the love and approval of the therapist. The patient will say and do anything the patient thinks the therapist wants in order to get the therapist's approval. Other vulnerable patients are those who have experienced trauma, which does compromise their ability to trust in their own reality. But the trauma they experienced was not childhood sexual abuse, or the abuse was not as extreme as they describe. It could have been intense neglect or other trauma that could dispose these patients to being swayed into believing that they had experienced childhood sexual abuse.

Some traditional analysts have attributed many reports of abuse to fantasies of an oedipal nature, resulting from eroticized transferences. It is important to differentiate eroticized transferences from actual reports of abuse. This may not be easy, because they can both be happening at the same moment. Reports of abuse can be used in the service of an eroticized transference. This can be complicated further if the analyst is encouraging this process because the patient's reports are meeting some voyeuristic and sexual needs of his or her own. Some patients who have not been sexually abused have presented material in a sexual way to get the needed attention they desire. These presentations may be expressions of preoedipal needs, and such situations may be more common between a female patient and a male therapist. The patient may actually feel too young emotionally for any sexual feelings in a genital sense, but may feel there is no other way of getting attention but through sexual appeal. This may be experienced by the therapist as a demand or a provocation rather than as an expression of a more subtle sexual awareness. The eroticized transference of a nonsexually abused patient will usually not exhibit the dissociative states one sees in the sexually abused patient.

Other therapist needs may affect the process, such that patients feel obligated to present the therapist with abuse material. For example, therapists who are abuse survivors themselves are more likely to see abuse in their patients, and may project their own experience onto the patient. A new, overzealous therapist may need to unearth dramatic and intense experiences in order to feel effective. Some colleagues of mine have described situations in which therapists with almost no information and a few vague symptoms have jumped to the conviction that the patient was sexually abused, and tried to convince the patient of this. These are examples of excesses that are damaging to the patient. If the patient is not a survivor of abuse, the therapist is undermining the patient's own sense of reality. If the patient is a survivor of abuse, then the therapist is trying to speed up the process by violating the patient's sense of control and self-pacing of the process.

Another type of situation occurs when patients feel that the therapist is not taking in the depth of their pain. In this case patients may concretize their pain in symbols. This then can lead to the literal acceptance of the symbol as the event.

Differentiating real abuse memories from fantasies requires the therapist to look at the patient's overall pattern of behavior. Terr (1991) delineated a very specific syndrome of symptomatology for a person who has experienced childhood trauma. In a sexual abuse victim one sees the full syndrome, which includes the following long-lasting symptoms: repeated perceived memories of the traumatic event (these can be bodily reexperiencing); repetitive behaviors related to the event; trauma-specific fears; and changed attitudes about people, life, and the future (i.e., fearfulness, pessimism, and not being connected to the future). Ann exhibited all four of these symptoms.

Terr specified three subgroups with even more specific symptom patterns. A Type I trauma syndrome is characterized by a single unanticipated traumatic event occurring in childhood, whereas Type II traumatic disorders are characterized by repeated exposure to extreme events. Type I syndrome is characterized by full detailed memories, omens (details of the trauma become warnings of coming disasters), and misperceptions. Type II symptoms include denial and numbing, self-hypnosis, dissociation, and rage. Although Ann did not exhibit the Type I symptoms, she did exhibit all of the Type II symptoms. The third subgroup is a crossover of both types, having symptoms of both Type I and II trauma. According to Terr, this third condition occurs after sudden, shocking deaths in the family, or accidents that leave the child handicapped. In addition, this group is characterized by considerable sadness. Terr pointed out that repetitive reenactment of the trauma refers to some exact detail of the original trauma, even if it is not recognized as such by the victim. This is true also for the specific fears of the patient, which are thought to correspond with the exact details of the trauma.

I have found that in my experience not all sexually abused patients fit perfectly into Terr's schema. But, again, I think it is a useful rule of thumb, rather than the absolute, as she portrays it.

I have begun to think about the unconscious as having different levels corresponding to the different types of memory described earlier in this chapter. The repressed memory controversy can possibly be, in part, an artifact of our not recognizing these different types of memories. This is complicated further by the presence of these many different types of memories in different dissociated self states. The goal of analysis is to understand and integrate these different levels of experience, memory, and self states into an integrated and articulate narrative of the self.

GUIDELINES AND CONCLUSIONS

Analysis and psychotherapy can help people in very powerful ways. The process should not be compromised by fears related to controversies, such as the false memory debate. Here are some guidelines that will help preserve the integrity of the therapeutic process.

A therapist is not a detective, a district attorney, a rescuer, or a companion. In my opinion, the role of a therapist is to help the person explore and develop his or her inner world, and experiment with how to relate to the outer world.

In general, therapists should follow the patient's ideas; they should listen to rather than tell the patient what he or she experienced. It is important not to get caught up in worrying about whether the material is true, because this will interfere with one's ability to listen and follow the patient's material. Patients' accounts of the traumatic events, in their view, explain their life. Withdrawing from the struggle about truth or falsehood allows patients to develop a narrative of their life. Patients may put the therapist on the spot and ask if the therapist believes them. In this situation, it may be best to think that patients feel that the depth of pain is unheard and unrecognized. Such patients may be asking the therapist to reflect back their pain and explore their feelings and hurt with them.

In situations, such as deciding whether to file a child abuse report, in which the therapist must have a reasonable suspicion that the abuse happened, one can use the existing literature for help. For example, the work of Terr (1991) and others can help determine whether the patient fits the syndrome of childhood trauma, and if the symptoms fit with the abuse being described. Is there external validation of the reports? Does the family pattern fit the profile of probable abusive families? Do the transference patterns resemble those described in the literature?

The field is always changing, and for many years false memory reports were extremely rare. They may be more frequent today, but in my opinion false reports of abuse are still relatively rare. One must be cautious in this increasingly hostile environment before recommending that the patient confront family members. The patient must be prepared for intense and hostile reactions, and there may be extreme consequences to these actions. These confrontations are where much acrimony begins and lawsuits start. If confrontation is necessary and a therapist is requested to assist, then it might be best to have another therapist conduct the confrontation session, or at least the person confronted needs to be given written warning. This warning should include discussion of the possibility that this confrontation will be very upsetting. The confronted persons need to know that you are not there for them and have no therapeutic duty to protect their interests. They should not pay for the session, which would set up a conflict of interest with the original patient.

When the therapist becomes involved in abuse-related lawsuits, the patient frequently feels betrayed, because in the legal system the therapist is put into a dual role of therapist and legal witness/expert. The therapist is forced by the opposing attorney to say and do things that the patient will probably experience as a betrayal. The patient may then sue the therapist for damaging his or her therapy and hurting the case. Lawsuits against therapists are skyrocketing, so the therapist should consult a lawyer if problems arise.

The research and literature on sexual abuse and its memories has become more sophisticated and can help us guide our way between the Scylla and Charybdis of trauma and false memories.

CHAPTER 17

Therapist Survival: Concluding Perspectives and Strategies

Even with the experiences of my patients and of my own life before me, I continue to experience cycles of belief and disbelief with respect to sexual abuse, ritual abuse, and dissociative disorders. The therapist's acknowledgment of these phenomena may threaten his or her affective needs and theoretical assumptions that concretize these needs. Dissociative disorders may challenge basic concepts of what constitutes a person. Sexual-abuse and ritual-abuse stories can be so horrific as almost to ensure countertransference problems.

To integrate the phenomena of trauma, sexual abuse, ritual abuse, and dissociative disorders, many therapists feel forced to leap across reality frames. This leap darkens therapists' views of human relationships, and can be frightening. Yet this integration may be essential in order to help many of these patients.

In this book, I have attempted to describe treatment from the therapist's and the patient's perspectives. Therapy is a process of mutual influence. It involves two people, one trying to get help and the other trying to give help, with all the foibles of people trying to work out a relationship. In the treatment process, therapists and patients must collaborate to open doors to hidden parts of patients' experience. This process may require therapists to open previously locked doors within themselves. Opening each door is at once an act of necessity and/or desperation, fear, curiosity, and courage.

On one side are the patients, who have been hurt and felt betrayed. Being believed is critical for most trauma patients because their experience of the validity of their right to exist, to have needs, to choose, and act has been damaged. The trauma is usually denied by the perpetrators and others around the victims, further undermining the patients' faith in their own perceptions. At the same time, these patients are extremely observant and perceptive, skills born of necessity for survival, and sense the distancing of others when they ask for help with their trauma.

On the other side are therapists, simultaneously aware of the patient's acute vulnerabilities and hopes for the therapist's help, and yet aware of their own powerlessness, at times, to prevent the patient's self-destruction. This duality challenges therapists' ability to consolidate an identity and a clear role. The tension between fears that therapists may cause their patients' deaths or suicides, and yet feel powerless to stop their enactments and self-destruction, can strain therapists.

STAGES AND DEVELOPMENTAL TASKS, AND THEIR EMOTIONAL DEMANDS

I have organized treatment around a set of stages and developmental tasks. Both participants need to be deeply aware of one another and of themselves at each step in order to explore the patient's openings or questions. This awareness evokes emotions and memories, which usually need to be explored to keep the process on track and bring healing.

Some fundamental coping strategies for therapists and patients are implicit once therapists understand the meaning of patients' questions. To at least comprehend the questions places both parties on more solid footing. A major source of information to use is the therapist's own feelings. That is why therapists' deeper awareness of their own experience will help them understand both parties.

In the first stage of treatment therapists need to consciously orient themselves, and the treatment techniques, to facilitate the patient's experience of safety, ability to think, and confidence in being heard. The therapist must not try to move the treatment too fast. These issues need to be dealt with as a foundation upon which the rest of treatment is built. The patient's anxiety and fear can be contagious, and the therapist needs to be able to stay calm and maintain the cohesion of the therapeutic role. The therapist needs to not take the patient's fear and defensive maneuvers as a personal injury. Patients depend on the therapist's ability to concretely problem solve, to take their fears seriously, and to help them feel safer and calmer.

In trying not to take the patient's behavior personally, I have found it helpful to try to create some distance from the overwhelming affects, in order to gain some perspective on the situation. I try to see beyond the defensive maneuver to the injured child inside the patient. This tends to increase my empathy and decrease power struggles with the patient. I find it helpful to encourage my curiosity and interest in learning about another person's world and experience. I explore which of the needs I have of patients are being frustrated, and which needs or events from my past are intruding into my interaction with patients. I ask myself, "Am I allowing my patients to be the people they are, or turning them into the traumatic experience from my own childhood?" This can involve turning the patient into a helpless victim who I need to save, or the perpetrator who mistreated or neglected me. If I can see what I am doing, then I can begin to disentangle myself from the past and deal more effectively with the patient.

Once the therapeutic situation is relieved of my own baggage, I can set more appropriate therapeutic boundaries and regain my empathy for the patient as a whole person. It is this combination of empathic understanding (for myself and for the patient), and reasonable and caring limits, that provides the context in which patients can work through their trauma in ways that create more maturity and integration. I have found that my fears of setting limits with patients usually have to do with my own fears of abandonment. When I allow patients to mistreat me, I become afraid of my building anger. Patients are not only needy, but competent and powerful agents in their own lives.

An element of the first stage of treatment is helping the patient to feel comfortable using the therapist as a selfobject or soothing helpful other, for whom the patient does not have to be a caregiver. The therapist is the caregiver. To provide this function, the therapist has to relinquish some need for acknowledgment and to be at center stage. With this support the patient can begin to explore in ways that were formerly too frightening.

This begins the second stage of treatment. Once patients feel comfortable using the therapist to help them function, they can take the therapist into their world. In this world there are many experiences patients cannot deal with and have not shared with any other person. These are what the therapist needs to take in, manage, and bear witness to. I have highlighted frequent areas that patients need help with: the traumatic experiences, patients' internalized sense of badness, the discontinuous experience of the self, the enactment of the trauma, their relationship to their body, and the possibility of ritual abuse.

Each of these areas requires therapists to immerse themselves in the patient's experience. Each requires therapists to more fully give up their own reality and personal anchors, and to enter a new world filled with pain. The patient's world involves realities that may or may not be familiar to the therapist. Some of these possibilities may threaten the therapist's worldview. To enter is to let go and to experience something new and something archaic, new in that this person will have had experiences the therapist has not, and archaic in that the patient's material will trigger in the therapist very personal experiences as well.

To let go in this way is both scary and exciting. Therapists need to let go into the patient's experience, and come back to their own center within themselves and their own experience. Some balance of going back and forth between these two centers of gravity is what enriches the process. Being too centered in one or another means either losing the patient or the therapist's own self.

Rigidity in either center interferes with treatment. Evelyn Schwaber (1983) has pointed out the effect of theory on the therapist's perceptions of the patient's material. The therapist's theoretical persuasion, however, is but one influence among many. Personal beliefs have a strong effect as well; therapists have an investment in maintaining their own belief system. This investment can, at times, impede the ability to hear and believe the patient or to see the openings to deeper experience. In treatment there is a continuous tension between the therapist's and the patient's needs.

One of the most difficult aspects in this treatment process is the periods of darkness. Therapists and patients may lose connection to hope. Amid the terror of their relived trauma, patients may feel the helplessness of the child dominated and controlled by others. These patients can be frozen in moments of the past with little to control the compulsion to enact their inner processes. At these moments patients need the therapist as a anchor outside of the compulsion to help them find a new way. The therapist needs to hold out the possibility of a new existence for the patient and be a solid transitional experience to this new way of being. In the midst of this the therapist may need some help. This book expresses the conviction that there is a model of treatment that, although arduous, can be effective for these patients, and is a guide for the therapist to manage the strain. Over the last few decades, our understanding of the treatment of these patients has changed dramatically for the better. The field has moved toward acceptance of dissociation as a major coping process, and is much more open to there being two subjectivities in the therapy room. The psychotherapeutic community accepts to a much greater extent that patients communicate to us on many levels, and that we hear aspects of this communication selectively. We must stay aware of how our experiences, expectations, and training affect this selection process, how this material is encoded, and meaning ascribed. Much of this happens automatically and preconsciously. Only if something does not fit our schemata do we become conscious of the process by which we decide the veracity of a patient's statement or the meaning of a patient's behavior. Therapists' abilities and personal and professional determination to stay aware are major safeguards.

THERAPIST SURVIVAL STRATEGIES

To stay whole, therapists need sustaining experiences outside the treatment of abused and traumatized patients, including professional support and a nourishing personal life. If any of these factors is missing, the risk increases that the intensity of the therapeutic process will take a deleterious toll on therapists and on their ability to treat their patients effectively.

I have had to consider how to balance my practice and avoid burnout while treating severely sexually abused and traumatized patients. I decided I need to either stay in therapy, be in supervision, or have a peer support group while treating these heavy cases. Today there are some supervisors who understand this process; this has not always been the case. When I started in this field over twenty years ago, I had great difficulty finding supervisors who could understand this treatment process. Recently I have discovered several colleagues and supervisors who have excellent competence in this area. In discovering them, I have learned that many of them have been on a similar path to mine, learning through first-hand experience, often alone and without support of others who had done it before us. Contact with these colleagues is very helpful. In addition, I try to have no more than two actively suicidal patients at a time, to limit sexual abuse cases to no more than one-half of my practice, and to limit late-night calls. I take a minimum of three weeks' vacation a year, go to conferences for professional stimulation, and participate in a study group with peers. I exercise, usually swimming or biking, and meditate to counteract all the sitting and frustration involved in my work. Managing stress and keeping optimally functional as a therapist is necessarily a daily process.

Even with this knowledge and perspective, sometimes I wonder if my career is an acting-out of my pathology. Then I remember the joy that I have felt when I have been able to help a damaged person heal and enjoy a rewarding life. I feel happy at the special intimacy I have had with those I have worked with in deep treatment. I have seen the vast differences between human minds. I have heard my patients' secret thoughts. This seems to compensate for the strain. I may still question myself when I get another midnight call, but usually in the morning it all feels worthwhile again.

References

Alexander, F. (1950). Conversion hysteria, vegetative neurosis, and psychogenic organic disturbance. In *Psychosomatic Medicine*, pp. 39–44. New York: W. W. Norton.
——— (1961). Analysis of therapeutic factors in psychoanalytic treatment. In *The Scope of Psychoanalysis: Selected Papers 1921–1961*. New York: Basic Books.
Bacal, H., and Thompson, P. (1996). The psychoanalyst's selfobject needs and the effect of their frustration on treatment. In *Progress in Self Psychology*, ed. A. Goldberg, pp. 17–35. Hillsdale, NJ: Analytic Press.
Beebe, B. (1993). *Infant research*. Paper presented at the Institute of Contemporary Psychoanalysis, Los Angeles, June.
Beebe, B., and Lachmann, F. (1988). Mother–infant mutual influence and precursors of psychic structure. In *Progress in Self Psychology*, vol. 3, ed. A. Goldberg, pp. 3–26. New York: Analytic Press.
Bowlby, J. (1988). *A Secure Base: Parent–Child Attachment and Healthy Human Development*. New York: Basic Books.
Brandchaft, B. (1988). *Critical issues in regard to empathy*. Presented

at the Eleventh Annual Conference on the Psychology of the Self, Washington, DC, October 16.

Breger, L. (1981). *Freud's Unfinished Journey: Conventional and Critical Perspectives in Psychoanalytic Theory.* London: Routledge & Kegan Paul.

Breuer, J., and Freud, S. (1893–1895). Studies on hysteria. *Standard Edition* 2:1–35.

Briere, J. (1992a). *Child Abuse Trauma: Theory and Treatment of the Lasting Effects.* Newbury Park, CA: Sage.

——— (1992b). Studying delayed memories of childhood sexual abuse. *The Advisor: American Professional Society on the Abuse of Children* (special issue) 5(3):17–18.

Bromberg, P. (1994). "Speak! that I may see you": some reflections on dissociation, reality and psychoanalytic listening. *Psychoanalytic Dialogues* 4(4):517–547.

Burland, J., and Raskin, R. (1990). The psychoanalysis of adults who were sexually abused in childhood: A preliminary report from the discussion group of the American Psychoanalytic Association. In *Adult Analysis and Childhood Sexual Abuse*, ed. H. Levine, pp. 35–41. Hillsdale, NJ: Analytic Press.

Calof, D. (1993). *Multiple Personality and Dissociation: Understanding Incest, Abuse, and MPD.* Park Ridge, IL: Parkside.

Clyman, R. (1992). The procedural organization of emotions: a contribution from cognitive science to the psychoanalytic theory of therapeutic action. In *Affect: Psychoanalytic Perspectives*, ed. T. Shapiro and R. Emde, pp. 349–382. Madison, CT: International Universities Press.

Cohen, J. (1985). Trauma and repression. *Psychoanalytic Inquiry* 5:163–189.

Curtis, R. (1993). *Psychoanalysis at the edge: the emerging model of motivation and mental organizing processes.* Paper presented at the annual meeting of the American Psychological Association, Toronto, Canada, August.

Davies, J. (1994). *Dissociation, repression and reality testing in the countertransference: the controversy over memory and false memory in adult incest survivors.* Paper presented at the 14th annual

Division 39 spring meeting of the American Psychological Association, Washington, DC, April.

Davies, J., and Frawley, M. (1992a). Dissociative processes and transference-countertransference paradigms in the psychoanalytically oriented treatment of adult survivors of childhood sexual abuse. *Psychoanalytic Dialogues* 2(1):5–36.

——— (1992b). Reply to Gabbard, Shengold, and Grotstein. *Psychoanalytic Dialogues* 2(1):77–96.

——— (1994). *Treating the Adult Survivor of Childhood Sexual Abuse: A Psychoanalytic Perspective*. New York: Basic Books.

Emde, R., Biringen, Z., Clyman, R., and Oppenheim, D. (1991). The moral self of infancy: affective core and procedure knowledge. *Developmental Review* 11:251–270.

Erikson, E. (1950). *Childhood and Society*. New York: W. W. Norton.

Faller, K. (1992). Can therapy induce false allegations of sexual abuse? *The Advisor: American Professional Society on the Abuse of Children* (special issue) 5(3):3–6.

Ferenczi, S. (1932). *The Clinical Diary of Sándor Ferenczi*, ed. J. Dupont. Cambridge, MA: Harvard University Press, 1985.

——— (1933). Confusion of tongues between adults and the child: the language of tenderness and passion. In *Final Contributions to the Problems and Methods of Psychoanalysis*, vol. 3, ed. M. Balint, pp. 156–167. New York: Basic Books, 1955.

Finkelhor, D., Hotaling, G., Lewis, I., and Smith, C. (1990). Sexual abuse in a national survey of adult men and women: prevalence, characteristics, and risk factors. *Child Abuse and Neglect* 14:19–28.

Fraiberg, S. (1959). *The Magic Years: Understanding and Handling the Problems of Early Childhood*. New York: Scribner's.

Freud, S. (1887–1902). *The Origins of Psycho-analysis, Letters to Wilhelm Fliess, Drafts and Notes: 1887-1902*, ed. M. Bonaparte, A. Freud, and E. Kris. New York: Basic Books, 1954.

——— (1896a). Heredity and the aetiology of the neuroses. *Standard Edition* 3:142–156.

——— (1896b). Further remarks on the neuro-psychoses of defense. *Standard Edition* 3:159–185.

—— (1896c). The aetiology of hysteria. *Standard Edition* 3:189–221.

—— (1900). The interpretation of dreams. *Standard Edition* 4–5:1–627.

Giovacchini, P. (1993). *Borderline Patients, the Psychosomatic Focus, and the Therapeutic Process.* Northvale, NJ: Jason Aronson.

Goldberg, A., ed. (1992). *New Therapeutic Visions: Progress in Self Psychology*, vol. 8. Hillsdale, NJ: Analytic Press.

Greenberg, J., and Mitchell, S. (1983). *Object Relations in Psychoanalytic Theory.* Cambridge, MA: Harvard University Press.

Grigsby, J., Schneiders, J., and Kaye, K. (1991). Reality testing, the self and the brain as modular distributed systems. *Psychiatry* 54:39–54.

Hamilton, V. (1989). The mantle of safety. In *Winnicott Studies*, ed. F. Tustin. no. 4, pp. 70–97.

Hanks, H., Hobbs, C., and Wynne, J. (1988). Early signs and recognition of sexual abuse in the pre-school child. *In Early Prediction and Prevention of Child Abuse*, ed. K. Browne, C. Davies, and P. Stratton, pp. 139–160. Chichester, England: John Wiley.

Herman, J. (1992). *Trauma and Recovery.* New York: Basic Books.

Herman, J., and Schatzow, E. (1987). Recovery and verification of childhood sexual abuse. *Psychoanalytic Psychology* 4:1–15.

Janet, P. (1889). *L'Automatisme Psychologique.* Paris: Alcan.

Kluft, R. (1984). Treatment of multiple personality disorder: a study of 33 cases. *Psychiatric Clinics of North America* 7:9–29.

—— (1991). Clinical presentations of multiple personality disorder. *Psychiatric Clinics of North America* 14(3):605–629.

Kohut, H. (1971). *The Analysis of the Self.* New York: International Universities Press.

—— (1977). *The Restoration of the Self.* New York: International Universities Press.

—— (1981). *Reflections on empathy.* Paper presented at the Self Psychology Meeting in Berkeley, CA, October.

—— (1984). *How Does Analysis Cure?* Chicago: University of Chicago Press.

Krull, M. (1986). *Freud and His Father.* New York: W. W. Norton.

Krystal, H. (1988). *Integration and Self Healing: Affect—Trauma— Alexithymia*. Hillsdale, NJ: Analytic Press.

Levine, H. (1990). *Adult Analysis and Childhood Sexual Abuse*. Hillsdale, NJ: Analytic Press.

Lichtenberg, J. (1983). *Psychoanalysis and Infant Research*. Hillsdale, NJ: Analytic Press.

Loewenstein, R., and Ross, D. (1992). Multiple personality and psychoanalysis: an introduction. *Psychoanalytic Inquiry* 12(1):3–48.

Loftus, E. (1992). The malleability of memory. *The Advisor: American Professional Society on the Abuse of Children* (special issue) 5(3):7–9.

Los Angeles Times Study (1985). Primary researchers: Timnick and Lewis. *Los Angeles Times*, August 25, A–1, A–34.

Maslow, A. (1962). *Towards a Psychology of Being*. Princeton, NJ: Van Nostrand.

Masson, J. (1984). *The Assault on Truth: Freud's Suppression of the Seduction Theory*. New York: Farrar, Straus, & Giroux.

Meiselman, K. (1978). *Incest: A Psychological Study of Causes and Effects with Treatment Recommendations*. San Francisco: Jossey-Bass.

Miller, A. (1979). *Prisoners of Childhood*. New York: Basic Books, 1981.

——— (1981). *The Drama of the Gifted Child: The Search for the True Self*. New York: Basic Books.

——— (1983). *For Your Own Good: Hidden Cruelty in Child-Rearing and the Roots of Violence*. New York: Farrar, Straus, & Giroux.

——— (1984). *Thou Shalt Not Be Aware: Society's Betrayal of the Child*. New York: Farrar, Straus, & Giroux.

——— (1988). *Banished Knowledge: Facing Childhood Injuries*. New York: Doubleday.

Miller, I. (1993). Ferenczi, RN, and the struggle for equal ground. *Journal of the American Academy of Psychoanalysis* 21(2):291–302.

Pearlman, L., and Saakvitne, K. (1995). *Trauma and the Therapist*. New York: W. W. Norton.

Perlman, S. (1993). Unlocking incest memories: preoedipal transference, countertransference, and the body. *Journal of the American Academy of Psychoanalysis* 21(3):363–386.

———— (1995). One analyst's journey into darkness: countertransference resistance to recognizing sexual abuse, ritual abuse, and multiple personality disorders. *Journal of the American Academy of Psychoanalysis* 23(1):137–151.

———— (1996a). "Reality" and countertransference in the treatment of sexual abuse patients: the false memory controversy. *Journal of the American Academy of Psychoanalysis* 24(1):115–135.

———— (1996b). Psychoanalytic treatment of chronic pain: the body speaks on multiple levels. *Journal of the American Academy of Psychoanalysis* 24(2):257–271.

Perry, N. (1992). How children remember and why they forget. *The Advisor: American Professional Society on the Abuse of Children* (special issue) 5(3):1–16.

Putnam, F. (1989). *Diagnosis and Treatment of Multiple Personality Disorder.* New York: Guilford.

———— (1991). The satanic ritual abuse controversy. *Child Abuse and Neglect* 15:175–179.

Rachman, A. (1989). Confusion of tongues: the Ferenczian metaphor for childhood seduction and emotional trauma. *Journal of the American Academy of Psychoanalysis* 17(2):181–205.

Reich, W. (1945). *Character Analysis.* New York: Simon & Schuster, 1972.

Russell, D. (1984). *Sexual Exploitation: Rape, Child Sexual Abuse and Workplace Harassment.* Newbury Park, CA: Sage.

Saywitz, K. (1992). Enhancing children's memory with the cognitive interview. *The Advisor: American Professional Society on the Abuse of Children* (special issue) 5(3):9–10.

Schafer, R. (1983). *The Analytic Attitude.* New York: Basic Books.

Schwaber, E. (1983) Psychoanalytic listening and psychic reality. *International Review of Psycho-Analysis* 10:379–392.

Searles, H. (1955). The informational value of the supervisor's emotional experiences. *Psychiatry* 18:135–146.

———— (1975). The patient as therapist to his analyst. In *Tactics and Techniques in Psychoanalytic Therapy, vol. 2: Countertransference,* ed. P. Giovacchini, pp. 95–151. New York: Jason Aronson.

Shane, M., Shane, E., and Gales, M. (1997). *Intimate Attachments: Toward a New Self Psychology*. New York: Guilford.

Shengold, L. (1989). *Soul Murder: The Effects of Childhood Abuse and Deprivation*. New York: Ballantine.

——— (1992). Commentaries on "Dissociative processes and transference-countertransference paradigms in the psychoanalytically oriented treatment of adult survivors of childhood sexual abuse." *Psychoanalytic Dialogues* 2(1):49–59.

Sinason, V. (1992). *Mental Handicap and the Human Condition: New Approaches from the Tavistock*. London: Free Association Press.

Spanos, N., and Borgess, C. (1994). Hypnosis, multiple personality disorders: a sociocognitive perspective. In *Dissociation*, ed. S. Lynn and J. Rhue, pp. 136–158. New York: Guilford.

Spitz, R. (1946). Anaclitic depression. *Psychoanalytic Study of the Child* 2:313–342. New York: International Universities Press.

Squire, L. (1986). Mechanisms of memory. *Science* 232:1612–1619.

——— (1987). *Memory and Brain*. New York: Oxford University Press.

Stern, D. (1985). *The Interpersonal World of the Infant: A View from Psychoanalysis and Developmental Psychology*. New York: Basic Books.

Stolorow, R. (1986). On experiencing an object: a multidimensional perspective. *Progress in Self Psychology* 2:273–279.

——— (1994). The nature and therapeutic action of psychoanalytic interpretation. In *The Intersubjective Perspective*, ed. R. Stolorow, G. Atwood, and B. Brandchaft, pp. 43–55. Northvale, NJ: Jason Aronson.

Stolorow, R., and Atwood, G. (1979). *Faces in a Cloud: Subjectivity in Personality Theory*. New York: Jason Aronson.

——— (1992). *Context of Being: The Intersubjective Foundations of Psychological Life*. Hillsdale, NJ: Analytic Press.

Stolorow, R., Brandchaft, B., and Atwood, G. (1987). *Psychoanalytic Treatment: An Intersubjective Approach*. Hillsdale, NJ: Analytic Press.

Sullivan, H. (1953). *The Interpersonal Theory of Psychiatry*. New York: W. W. Norton.

Terr, L. (1990). *Too Scared to Cry: Psychic Trauma in Childhood.* New York: HarperCollins.

——— (1991). Childhood trauma: an outline and overview. *American Journal of Psychiatry* 148(1):10–20.

——— (1994). *True memory of childhood trauma: the quirks, absences and returns.* Paper presented at the American Psychological Association convention, Los Angeles, August.

van der Kolk, B., and Fisler, R. (1994). Childhood abuse and neglect and loss of self-regulation. *Bulletin of the Menninger Clinic* 58(2):145–168.

van der Kolk, B., McFarlane, A., and Weisaeth, L. (1996). *Traumatic Stress: The Effects of Overwhelming Experience on Mind, Body, and Society.* New York: Guilford.

Williams, L. (1992). Adult memories of childhood abuse: preliminary findings from a longitudinal study. *The Advisor: American Professional Society on the Abuse of Children* (special issue) 5(3):19–21.

Winnicott, D. W. (1947). Hate in the countertransference. In *D. W. Winnicott: Collected Papers*, pp. 194–203. New York: Basic Books.

——— (1972a). The capacity to be alone. In *The Maturational Processes and the Facilitating Environment*, pp. 29–36. New York: International Universities Press.

——— (1972b). Ego distortion in terms of true and false self. In *The Maturational Processes and the Facilitating Environment*, pp. 140–152. New York: International Universities Press.

——— (1972c). Ego integration in child development. In *The Maturational Processes and the Facilitating Environment*, pp. 56–63. New York: International Universities Press.

Wright, L. (1993) Remembering Satan. *New Yorker*, May 17, pp. 61–80; May 24, pp. 54–76.

Young, W., Sachs, R., Braun, B., and Watkins, R. (1991). Patients reporting ritual abuse in childhood: a clinical syndrome. Report of 37 cases. *Child Abuse and Neglect* 15:181–189.

Index